Farmhouse
on the Edge of Town

Also from Islandport Press

Moon in Full
Marpheen Chann

The Ghosts of Walter Crockett
W. Edward Crockett

Dear Maine
Morgan Rielly and Reza Jalali

Bald Eagles, Bear Cubs, and Hermit Bill
Ron Joseph

Whatever It Takes
May Davidson

Hauling by Hand
Dean Lawrence Lunt

This Day in Maine
Joseph Owen

Downeast Genius
Earl Smith

Comfort is an Old Barn
Amy Calder

And Poison Fell From the Sky
MarieThérèse Martin

Farmhouse
on the Edge of Town

Stories from a Bed & Breakfast
in the Mountains of Western Maine

LEW-ELLYN HUGHES

ISLANDPORT  PRESS

ISLANDPORT PRESS

Islandport Press
P.O. Box 10
Yarmouth, Maine 04096
www.islandportpress.com
info@islandportpress.com

First Edition: November 2024
Printed in the United States of America.
All photographs, unless otherwise noted, courtesy of Lew-Ellyn Hughes.

ISBN: 978-1-952143-22-9
Library of Congress Control Number: 2022932037

Dean L. Lunt | Editor-in-Chief, Publisher
Shannon Butler | Vice President
Marion Fearing | Assistant Editor
Emily Lunt | Book Designer

This book is dedicated to the people of Maine's small towns, especially the wonderful people of Eustis and Stratton—those hardy Mainers who not only live Maine stories, they are Maine stories. For the years I lived among them, I will be forever grateful.

Table of Contents

SUMMER

FALL

Me, enjoying one of my favorite winter activities.

Prologue

In the late 1990s, my youngest daughter, Holland, and I were living in a crowded townhouse complex in the Eastern Maine city of Bangor. By this time, my two older daughters, Emily and Kelly, who were seven and nine years older than Holland respectively, were out on their own. I had been divorced for six years and I primarily worked as a medical records assistant for a state agency. The job paid my bills, but it was a desk job, just pushing papers, and on many days I had to grasp the seat of my chair and hang on for dear life to keep myself there. Although I did appreciate the job and my townhouse home, it was not a good fit.

I was not content.

I grew up living near cities, and I now wanted to live in a small town in the mountains. I wanted to see mountains and trees when I looked out my window, not buildings and concrete and the neighbor's dog pooping in the yard. That discontent motivated me to make a change—a big change. My upbringing taught me that you can do anything you wish to do if you have a heart of courage and you reach out and try to grasp what you want with both hands.

I wanted to live in a place like Stratton, a sweet little town roughly a two-hour drive from Bangor that finishes along Route 27 in Western Maine. It is surrounded by woods, wildlife, and mountains. I had been to Stratton a few times, hiking the area's mountain trails or skiing nearby at Sugarloaf, the state's largest ski resort, and increasingly found myself in that area.

Most of all, Stratton was full of space and peace, and on every trip I passed a rundown, abandoned 1890s farmhouse on the edge of town. I admired its lines, the wraparound porch, the three chimneys, and the huge barn. Sometimes I stopped to look at the property. I loved the way the brook sounded as it flowed by the yard on its way to the lake. I liked the log fence along the bank. I could see what was once a garden. I wondered about the history of this house. Eventually, on each trip back to Bangor, I pulled my car over, looked back sadly, and silently said goodbye to that farmhouse, the little village, and the majestic Bigelow Mountain Range rising up behind it.

After months of such goodbyes, I had an idea—maybe I should buy the farmhouse and turn it into a bed-and-breakfast. Yes, I understood that fixing it up was a huge undertaking. I ordered five books on how to own and operate a Bed-and-breakfast. It sounded rewarding. But it also sounded like a lot of work—a lot of all-consuming work. I put the idea on hold and stayed put in Bangor.

It all changed one evening—a short-staffed, full-moon chaos of an evening—while working at my second job as an evening charge nurse at a local long-term facility. I was comforting the family of a dying patient, although I knew there was a doctor on the phone, waiting to speak to me. Suddenly, a nursing assistant came running down the hall. She called out, "Mr. Smith crawled over his bed guard rail, fell onto the floor, and now his leg looks funny!" As I dashed down the hall to Mr. Smith's room, I clearly remember thinking, "Maybe running a bed-and-breakfast wouldn't be all that difficult."

The next week, I bought the 1890s farmhouse in Stratton.

Although my ancestors lived in Maine, I was born in Rancho Cordova, California. That said, I am not, by any stretch of the imagination, a California girl. But since *Summer Days*, the classic

1965 Beach Boys album my mother played, hyped the glory of being one, I claimed the fame. Whenever asked about my birthplace, I would proudly say, "I'm a California girl."

As I aged beyond the single digits of childhood, I realized I had nothing to do with the state of California and it had nothing to do with me. It was merely happenstance—California was just where one of my father's adventures had taken our family.

My father was an adventurer—a military man. We, my parents and my five siblings, moved around the country, and Canada, as his job required. In the mid 1950s, he and my mother packed up and left their hometown of Greenville, Maine, to travel the world, dragging their children (they eventually had six) through states and escapades.

Papa was a navigator, but he decided early in his career that if he was going up in an airplane, he was going to be in charge. So off we all went to Oklahoma where Papa attended pilot school. As scarce and scant as my memories of that place are, I clearly remember entering our tiny Oklahoma apartment for the first time. When I opened the refrigerator, it was empty, and that empty refrigerator left a strong impression. We would, of course, fill it with food and drink after we began living there, but I think back on that initial image as a metaphor for what our lives were like at each new place—empty until we filled them with new experiences.

The summer I turned five years old, my parents started taking us back to their hometown of Greenville. Every summer for the rest of my childhood we drove to Maine and stayed at a family camp on Moosehead Lake that my great-grandfather had built—it was the third cabin built on Harfords Point, a place that now has hundreds of homes. They took us back to Maine so that we, according to Papa, "would have roots." My father felt too many military children didn't have an awareness of their homeland or their heritage, and he wanted us to have that. We fell in love with Maine, which did, indeed, have deep family roots.

During our travels around America and beyond, I walked on battlegrounds, explored canyons, and wandered on Southern plantations. I fell off of Robert E. Lee's grandson's raised grave and have a scar on my shin to remind me. We never took the highway—we always traveled the back roads because that is where real life is. We lived like the locals lived and ate what the locals ate.

I was seven when Papa put me on downhill skis for the first time. We were living in Goose Bay, Labrador, for the longest period of time I had ever lived in one place—four years.

I was also seven and also living in Goose Bay the Christmas my father left on a mission and we had to delay our holiday festivities. He was an Air Force pilot flying SAR (search and rescue), and he left at midnight on Christmas Eve for an emergency air evacuation. He was gone all night and most of the next day, and Mama decided it would build character in us if our Christmas celebration was postponed until he returned home. I could understand that, but most of the bricks in this character building began to crumble when, although Papa made it home safe and sound by noon, we were forced to continue postponing the opening of our gifts until after a lengthy dinner at the Officer's Club and a seemingly never-ending trip down the yellow brick road in a mandatory viewing of *The Wizard of Oz*.

A few weeks later, I learned the details of his trip. Papa left his family in an old World War II C-54 to fly Sophie, an indigenous woman suffering a cerebral hemorrhage, to a hospital in Montreal, where she received life saving treatment. The air that night was twenty-nine below zero, with heavy ice and turbulence. The flight was slow going and long—longer than the movie I fussed about watching and longer than the dinner hour I whined through. Indeed, because he left at midnight, his trip was longer than the hours I was awake waiting for him. But I didn't know that then—I wasn't supposed to know—I was a kid waiting for *my* Christmas presents. He never spoke in his own defense.

I do remember the gift I was given that year, though, the gift of learning the true meaning of Christmas—it's about a hero.

My childhood was full of so many lessons.

One of our other stops was in Charleston, South Carolina, also a long way from Greenville, Maine. We lived in a home on the military base, and I was bussed ten miles to an inner-city, previously all-black high school during the desegregation of southern schools. It wasn't the original desegregation (I'm not that old!), it was the secondary integration of schools naturally segregated by neighborhoods.

The bus ride was long and confining. Some days were fearful. There were riots and vandalism. My bus was turned over, and I remember feeling indignant about that. There were cops and gangs and grumblings. There was a shooting in the parking lot. Much of the chaos was caused by malcontents from elsewhere fighting against integration. My parents refused an alternative for me that many of my peers' parents choose—private school. Instead, my father put me on the bus saying, "This is history; go live it." He was right. I enjoyed high school, learned so much more than reading, writing, and arithmetic, and continue to enjoy valued friendships from those times to this day

At the same time, I was *living* history, I was also *living* a double or oddly split life. During the three seasons of the year we lived in Charleston, not only was I bussed to an inner-city high school, I also attended etiquette classes so I could also fit in alongside Southern ladies as we attended the theater—complete with evening gowns and elbow-length white gloves. These classes were also important so I knew how to act like a proper lady when I danced with military officers-to-be at the Citadel. No doubt my mother hoped I'd find a future husband on the dance floor, especially since my teenage

5

tastes in boys tended more toward good ol' boys and Harley dudes than military officers.

And then during the fourth season, summer, my dancing shoes—actually all of my shoes—came off and I ran barefooted like a wild woodland nymph in the woods of Maine and beside the waters of Moosehead Lake. I discovered, while I felt comfortable acting like either Scarlett O'Hara or Fly Rod Crosby, it was the Maine woods that I loved. I learned to water ski, to navigate a boat, and to sail. With snorkel and goggles, Papa took me to the bottom of Moosehead Lake, and with backpack and boots, he took me to the top of Katahdin.

Finally, when my father retired from military service, we officially moved north to live in that old family camp on Moosehead, which had been renovated into a year-round home. I settled into a more routine life. I graduated from Greenville High School, went to nursing school, got married, hiked sections of the Appalachian Trail, raised three daughters, helped run the office at a log-home company, and eventually, after going through a divorce, I found myself working in nursing in Bangor. I once co-piloted a plane with my father over Moosehead Lake. He turned the controls over to me and, after a few moments, asked me if I knew where I was going. I smiled and said, "I have no idea, but this is amazing!"

Which is how I could describe my plans later in life. And I definitely felt the same way about opening a bed-and-breakfast in that old farmhouse on the edge of town. I had no idea what I was doing, but it was going to be amazing.

I hoped.

WINTER

Because of a Pig

I sometimes like to tell people I *really* moved to Stratton because of a pig. Actually, I moved to the northwestern mountains of Maine because of a pig's lifestyle. This little piggy got to live in a small town surrounded by mountains and forests and friendly people. He had it pretty good, this pig, and I wanted what he had—a simple life.

At the time, my youngest daughter, Holland, and I were living in Bangor where I worked as a medical records assistant and an evening charge nurse at a long-term care facility. I wasn't happy with the jobs or the city. One morning, I opened the curtain in our town house, only to see a big-bellied, scantily clad neighbor across the courtyard doing the same. Holland, who was twelve years old at the time, sighed deeply and said, "Mom, I'm ready for a new view."

"Me too," I said, as I raised my coffee cup in a morning greeting to the neighbor we had never met.

A year later, I was crawling underneath a barn in Stratton, praying the property would fall into my hands and not on my head. I noticed something in the far corner. I picked my way through mounds of discarded chicken wire, hay, and rotten lumber to what turned out to be a pig's pen. Large green painted letters on the door proclaimed "Pig." That was it. Just "Pig." There was a time when life in this place was so uncomplicated the owners didn't bother to name their pig. He or she—for without a name I will never know which—was simply Pig.

Now that's simple, I thought. And my decision was plain and simple; this was where I wanted to be.

It was perfect.

So soon there we were, me and my teenage daughter, living in an old farmhouse in the mountains, in a place where hoofprints outnumbered footprints. We were living in a setting where life's pressures were lessened by the frequent release of steam from our mouths into the fresh mountain air as we hiked the steep trails, skied the slopes, or paddled the waters around us. We loved this place that was so profoundly quiet that sometimes the only thing we heard was—nothing.

Although living at the old farmhouse would certainly prove challenging, I knew I'd rather battle the deer gnawing in my garden bed than the annoying traffic, and I preferred the noise from big-rig engine brakes than break-ins. These winding country roads were trickier than Interstate 95, but they always led me straight home. I knew my neighbors, yet I saw them not from across a courtyard, but at the market across the street where we could stop and visit with each other for a moment or two. We looked out our window to watch beavers swimming in the brook, deer pruning the raspberry bushes, and coyotes eating the apples that fell from the tree. And with this new view that we craved, our view of the rest of the world pretty much changed, too.

Thus began my journey, my life in a tiny town in the mountains of Western Maine, in an 1890s farmhouse-turned-bed-and-breakfast-and-bakery.

It's where I became a writer.

All because of a pig.

Crooked as an Old Witch's Spine

The farmhouse was as crooked as an old witch's spine. Her windows were so drafty, they gave the curtains wings. The floors creaked, the banisters wobbled, the roof leaked. Still, in my heart, she was beautiful and full of promise. I was captivated by her charm, her history, her potential. And, best of all, she sat on an acre of land on the edge of a brook that fed into Maine's fourth largest lake, next to a vast wilderness, just down the road from some massive mountains, in a small town in western Maine. She was where I wanted to be.

When I was preparing to buy the house, I hired a building inspector, and the first thing he did was fall through the rotten boards on the porch floor. He pulled himself out, dusted off his clothes, shrugged at me, and continued. I liked this guy. He looked the home over, and when he couldn't tell me anything I didn't already know or suspect, I was ready to buy the 1890s farmhouse.

As soon as it was officially mine, I got to work. At the top of the list was starting at the bottom of the house. Her old bones needed straightening. I hired a house-leveling company. They jacked the farmhouse and the barn to their upright positions and repaired the foundation to keep it so.

An aerial view of my farmhouse on the edge of town.

The house was now straight and sure, and she looked oh so much more respectful, like a lady of upright upbringing. But the plaster walls rebelled and cracked at the change. They were happy where they had settled in their old age. At night, as I lay in bed, I could hear portions of walls fall to the floor. I played a guessing game, trying to decipher which room was shedding the plaster of the past: The living room? The kitchen? The library? It became my morning ritual to put the coffee on and, while it perked, sweep up the dusty mess made overnight.

11

I couldn't hammer a nail in straight, so I had little to do with the renovations, but I certainly became a pro at demolition. I pulled horsehair and plaster off the walls for hours and days and while doing so, found some interesting things—like the saw placed in between the studs over the kitchen door. It was common practice for builders of the time to place one there upon completion of their job as a way to bring luck and prosperity to the home and keep evil spirits away. I left the saw in place, and I imagine it is still there.

After the electrician replaced the antiquated knob-and-tube wiring with updated electrical lines, new insulation and walls went in. In between renovation projects, I rented the rooms at a discounted price. Most people were fascinated, impressed even, at this project, but occasionally a guest or two, upon looking around and noticing this was a work in process, appeared worried about their stay. After assuring them that no construction would take place during their visit and that their room was perfectly perfect, they relaxed. I never wondered what I had gotten myself into, because I had renovated several homes before this one and worked as a construction coordinator for a log home company, but I could tell that a guest was wondering what she had walked into when she saw the stairway wall torn down to its studs. I joked and told her the wall was torn apart because I thought I heard a spider in there. She smiled and sighed in relief.

I was also creative with remodeling. I used the old doors that were in the barn as the ceiling in my office space. When it was time to replace the porch, I used the old, yet still solid porch posts as the window and door trim in one of the bedrooms. I told a friend that I had lived with paint color swatches tacked to the walls throughout the house for so long that I didn't think it would feel like home without one. That friend painted the second story hallway wall as a giant color swatch complete with paint names and numbers on the side.

When it was time to have the maple floors sanded and sealed, I moved out and stayed with a friend. The summer that all the walls were to be sheet rocked and painted, I shut the B&B down and took a job at the local campground as manager. But soon, the old house would be renewed and would grow to become a successful, full-time passion that consumed all my days and many of my nights as I waited up for late arrivals or slept with one eye open in case a guest needed something.

After the guests departed each day, after the breakfast dishes were washed, the beds remade, after the house was cleaned and ready for new visitors, there was always enough time to get outside, into the woods for a hike, a challenging mountain bike ride, or into my kayak for a scenic, relaxing paddle. In this new life of mine there was always enough time to breathe. It was perfect.

God gave us two feet for a reason: so we can balance on one with all we have learned in life, all we have experienced in our past, as we step out into the future with the other.

Diamond Corner
Bed & Breakfast

When I bought the farmhouse, which was located at the corners of Routes 16 and 27 in Stratton, some locals told me the name of the corner had always been Diamond Corner, but nobody seemed to know why. I immediately loved the name. Not only was it not alphabetically challenged for marketing purposes, but also, "a diamond in the rough" would be the perfect slogan for a luxury bed-and-breakfast in the rough wilderness of western Maine. Diamond Corner Bed & Breakfast: A Diamond in the Rough.

Perfect.

Several years later, a woman from the local historical society told me the truth about Diamond Corner. Diamond was a woman from way back in the beginning of the town's history—she was the town prostitute, and the corner was where she solicited her customers. This was her corner: Diamond's Corner.

Perfect.

My First Guests

While my first guests did not arrive until January 2002, I was actually supposed to entertain them the first week of October 2001. They were moose hunters. One of them was an older gentleman who, after years of trying, finally got his moose permit. He and three of his close friends were going to stay at the B&B and hunt. Although we had not yet completed the renovations, the farmhouse was still lovely and I was ready for them. And then one of the hunters died the weekend before their scheduled arrival.

Friends tried to console me by saying things like, "If the guy was going to die, it's better he wasn't here. You would always be known as 'that place where the first guest died.'"

A male friend agreed, adding, "You would be known as Diamond Corner Dead and Breakfast."

Horrible, I know, but they were trying to lighten the moment. Still, I slapped him.

A third friend gave her opinion. "I'm sorry for your disappointment, but, if it's any consolation, there is a perfect accounting system in the universe, everything happens for a reason. Apparently, in the big scheme of things, it was better that a man should die, than a moose should die."

Another friend summed up the third friend's thought thusly: the moose had connections.

A diamond in the rough!

I started wondering if it was an omen, but decided since there was nothing I could do about such a strange beginning, that I should simply get back to work, do my best and give it my all, as well as all my prayers. Finally, by January, my first real guests arrived. We were off and running.

The B&B had five bedrooms, a living room, a dining room and a lovely sitting room with a fireplace. (I would eventually build an addition to create a second story luxurious bathroom with a clawfoot tub and a laundry room. The first floor of the addition was my office, a mud room, and a storage area. My new office had a wall of windows that overlooked the large backyard and the garden.)

The rooms were lovely, all named and themed: Weeds had a garden decor; For Rest was like walking into a woodland cabin; Sea Whip was decorated like a seaside cottage; and Kim's Room was named for a dear friend and decorated to celebrate friendship. The fifth bedroom was Holland's private room. I slept wherever the guests did not. The farmhouse was uniquely decorated, cozy and welcoming.

Diamond Corner was a traditional European-style homestay, meaning guests were welcome to use the entire home. There were special touches like a tea table in the dining room where guests could help themselves to coffee, tea, or hot chocolate.

I finally entertained my first real live first guests on January 18, 2002—roughly six months to the day after I bought the property.

As time went on, my most frequent guests at Diamond Corner were people from cities in the northeast. The second most common visitors came from Europe, followed by guests from Canada. However, over the years, I hosted guests from around the world—from France to Romania to Germany to Italy to Ireland.

I also hosted Appalachian Trail hikers, Northern Forest Canoe Trail paddlers, and people on summer road trips. A few business folks stayed as well, and they appreciated the large oak desk in the library on which to work. One was a private detective for an out-of-state company who was in Stratton on assignment. I was curious, and he was willing to share. His job was to investigate an employee's claim of a back injury—an injury serious enough that the employee claimed he could not walk. The detective followed the man to a snowmobile trailhead, then watched (and recorded) him getting on a snowmobile and driving away. Case closed. It was too late in the day for the detective to drive back to New York, so he rented a room and was sitting at the oak desk in the library, filing his report, pen in one hand, cup of tea in the other as we chatted.

The open European-style home led to afternoons like the one I summed up in a letter to my daughter Emily:

"The guests have been rained off the mountain and now fill the library, dining room, and living room. This doesn't bother me; it's comfortable with them here. They are reading books from the library shelves, drinking tea, putting together jigsaw puzzles or watching movies. I think our newest board game Sequence will no doubt find its way to the dining room table; it usually does. One of the guests obviously feels quite at home here because she just yelled at the television.

"Amos the cat is earning his keep. He slept on the feet of a guest the other night, so he does have a job here. Jim, the guest, didn't mind of course—he could have shooed Amos out of his room, but instead invited him to keep his feet warm like his cat at home is in the habit of doing.

"One of the advertisements for the B&B reads: 'If you love homespun quilts on deeply comfortable featherbeds, toasty toes in cozy slippers, the smell of cinnamon and spice, fresh mountain air, and peaceful nights in a country farmhouse in the mountains . . . then you are going to love it here at Diamond Corner B&B.'

"And people certainly do.

"A guest just came into the kitchen, placed the *Maine Gazetteer* that I keep in the library on the counter, pointed to the northern Maine wilderness lake Caucomgomoc, and asked, "How do you pronounce that?"

"'Cock Mo Gom Moc,' I told him.

"'How do you know that?' he wanted to know.

"'I lived in an off-grid cabin on the shore of that lake, before off-grid was popular.'

"You wouldn't remember that, of course, since you were a baby and your sister a toddler. I didn't go into those details with him. By the look on his face, I didn't think he would believe me, and I don't have time or inclination to find the pictures to prove it."

One woman summed up the bed-and-breakfast nicely: "I always wanted my home to look like this, to be this warm and cozy and inviting, but I know it never will, so I'll just come here and pretend."

Usually, while my guests made themselves at home, I remained in the kitchen warmed by the woodstove, my oven full of breakfast bread, and my heart full of my love for this life.

Welcome Winter

At three o'clock this morning, I heard a snowplow scraping the road, a log truck whose driver was obviously proud of his engine brakes, and several pickup trucks splashing through the puddles created by the overnight rain. I even heard a horn honk, and personally, I think that is just downright rude before sunup.

My disturbed subconscious kicked off the cover of sleep and I awoke to a room, a house, and a world of peaceful silence. The noises had been a dream! The only traffic jam was the one in my head. I wasn't able to go back to sleep, so I gave in and got up. A day can't hold much promise when your second thought is "I wonder if I can squeeze in a two-hour nap after breakfast."

By sunrise, the rain had turned to snow, and the view out my windows was lovely—the backyard was an undisturbed blanket of snow laid before a black-and-gray forest of leafless, powdered trees. The side yard was a Christmas-card picture of the village: one washed in white and just coming to life. The folks who were already up were walking with their heads down and their collars up, protecting those tender spots—eyeballs and backbones—from falling snowflakes. I couldn't think of anything that brings on a shiver faster than a beautiful winter storm not viewed from a warm place within, or fresh snow finding its way down your back.

Outside my kitchen window high-bush cranberries dangled from a limb, and as I admired the stark contrast of the red-hot berries against the white cold of winter, I noticed a "berry" slight movement. The berries seem to be giggling. They had a secret, and although they remained hush-hush on their bush, their bellies jiggled in merriment. Perhaps they knew, having lived through the harvest and avoided my jelly jars, that they might survive the winter and they were chuckling to themselves with delight. Yes, we will survive the season—the berries have spoken.

I have a friend who lives in the south. She wrote to me this morning, boasting that the backs of her legs were warmed by the sun as she strolled through her neighborhood.

The backs of my legs were also warmed, not by the sun, which I hadn't seen in a few days, but by the fire in my kitchen Round Oak woodstove. Feeding the fire warms my heart as much as my extremities while I start my day. As a matter of fact, the fronts of

Wintertime at the bed-and-breakfast.

my legs are warmed too, by the cat that does figure eights through them nearly nonstop until I accidentally kick him when I turn to reach for another piece of wood, forcing him to swallow his pride and belly up to the dog for companionship.

Let my friend have her year-round summer. I love Maine winters. I like the feel of my toes in wool socks. I like fleece, flannel, fur, and footies.

Now, having said that, let me say I indulge in a spring runoff just about the time the mountain snow does the same. While the melting snow turns Maine into a mud bath, I can be found basking in the Florida sunshine. Taking refuge in the south from Maine's mud-laden spring does not mean I feel the same about Maine's winters. I like my mountains the way I like my doughnuts—sugared—and the blanket that warms me the most is the freshly fallen blanket of snow.

The days are cleaner, the nights are clearer, and the air is crisper. I think icy conditions bring people closer; cuddling just isn't the same in July as it is in January.

The garden is empty, the root cellar is full, the preserves and the thermostat are up. The nights are long enough for more than one chapter of a good book; the mercury is short enough for wool.

Bring it on, winter. You are welcome here.

Imagine

When I was a little girl I had a big plan. It was a simple blueprint of my future, and I had every reason to believe it would come to fruition because I didn't have a reason to believe it wouldn't. I was going to find and marry a man with the last name of Tenth. (All little girls know marrying the mate of your dreams is as easily accomplished as having the dream in the first place.) Mr. Tenth and I would have three beautiful daughters named April, May, and June and they would each, by miracle or cesarean section, be born on the tenth of the month for which they were named.

Imagine this conversation:

"What is your name?"

"April Tenth."

"When is your birthday?"

"April tenth."

"Really? What are your sisters' names?"

"May Tenth and June Tenth."

"Born on May and June tenth, I suppose?"

"Natch."

My best friend at the time, Candy Kane, agreed it was a wonderful idea. It was a naive plan fashioned out of childish cleverness. All I had to do was grow up.

And grow up I did.

I gave birth to three beautiful daughters, and today as I was looking at the youngest, Holland, it struck me like a ping pong ball to the side of my head that her birthday is indeed April tenth, which I've always known, but I had forgotten the significance of the date.

The day this child was born I could have easily told the hospital clerk that her last name was Tenth, and therefore made it so, but being under the influence of opiates and maturity, I let her family name stand and named her Holland, not April.

What was I thinking? It is obvious I wasn't thinking with a child's mind anymore. I was thinking with the responsible mind of an adult.

Why do childhood dreams vanish? Does the onset of adulthood mean the end of our dreams and our hopes that, when we were little, were as big as the sky and as free as the birds that call it home? Do our thoughts, like fallen stars, plummet to earth the further away from the ground we grow?

Do they get lost in the practicality of maturity? When we are children we are brave enough to dream of doing the impossible and unquestioning enough to believe there is no such thing as the unachievable. We walk around, innocent believing-in-everything souls who can do anything and be anything until we are sent to school where we are taught the laws of probability, nature, relativity, and accidental truths. It seems the more we grow, the more we know, and the less we believe in the measureless possibilities found only in one's untrained, unchained, childlike mind.

While I was pondering all this, I had a thought—it is not the child's mind, but the adult's mind that is flawed. Maybe this explains why an elderly person's thought processes often revert back to a childhood. Perhaps the aged, having come to the end of life, have also come to the conclusion that allowing the limited ideas of a responsible adult to govern one's life can be bland and boring. The old have grown wise and have therefore returned to the freedom that the whimsical thoughts of youth offer and in doing so have not lost their minds, but found them.

Imagine.

The Life of a
Bed-and-Breakfast Hostess

Many of my guests tell me I'm living their dream. I smile, but all the while I think, *I'm not going to tell you what hard work your dream is, in case I want to sell this place to you one day.*

One winter evening the water heater decided to quit. In a panic, I called the repairman.

"Help me!" I cried. "I own Diamond Corner Bed-and-breakfast in Stratton, I have a house full of guests, and my hot water heater just broke down!"

"Ma'am, is this an emergency?" the technician asked.

"Let me repeat myself," I said through clenched teeth. "I own a bed-and-breakfast. I have a full house of paying guests who just returned from a day on the ski slopes and will very soon want hot showers, and I don't have any hot water."

I took a breath, and unlike the water temperature, my voice rose. "I don't know what you consider an emergency, but I think this is fairly serious."

He arrived shortly and fixed the stubborn thing.

There was the time eight guests had just settled in at the breakfast table and my oven played copycat to the hot water heater—it decided not to ignite. After scrambling for other ingredients, I made eggs, and nobody was the wiser that the original menu called for cinnamon French toast soufflé with a maple-nutmeg sauce.

The problems at the bed-and-breakfast could range from a broken range to Easter Bunny table centerpieces that refused to stay upright and needed to be duct-taped in place. Believe me, the bed-and-breakfast had come with a complete working set of monkey wrenches.

My life as a hostess was one of loosely constrained panic with intermittent bouts of paranoia, followed by several days of exhaustion before it started all over again. My guests thought my laugh was social when more often it was borderline sociopathic.

Some of the guests asked odd questions that amazed, amused, or alarmed me.

One woman called and demanded, "Tell me what you serve and I'll tell you if my kids will eat it."

Fortunately, my B&B just happened to be full the night of her requested stay.

One of my guest rooms, called Kim's Room.

Another, during the check-in tour, asked, "Which bedroom is yours?"

"All of them," I told her.

A woman from Illinois called and wanted to know if I was on the route to Maryland. I told her my business is in Maine.

She was doubtful.

"Maine?" she asked. "Is that a state?"

Very few things left me speechless, but I realized that was the case this time when I heard her say, "Hello? Hello? Are you there?"

There were some people who never got to stay with me, but from our phone conversations alone, I wish I could have met them face to face. Pete was a perfect example. He called one Friday morning during the height of snowmobile season to see if I had availability for the weekend. I did. He was excited about his brand-new snowmobile and was eager to get on the trails. Before he could reserve the room for Friday night, however, he needed to take care of a loose end.

Pete called me back to say he wouldn't be arriving until Saturday morning because that loose end—his wife—was still on the loose and he had to find her to tell her he was going to Eustis snowmobiling for the weekend. Early Saturday morning Pete called again. In a downtrodden tone, he let me know he would not be coming at all—he'd found his wife.

The most typical reasons reservations are canceled are illness or work, but one woman canceled because, according to her, "Guys are such jerks!" I didn't ask.

One gentleman who thoroughly enjoyed hearing about my funny and interesting guests wondered if I would share stories about the not-so-wonderful.

"Who has been your worst guest?" he asked.

His wife patted his arm and with a gentle voice warned him, "Dear, you haven't left yet."

Another one of my guest rooms, this one called Sea Whip.

When there were guests in my home, there was never a dull moment. I've jump-started a Harley, called the paramedics, babysat a parakeet, fixed the bed that a little monkey jumped on, and argued with moose-searching visitors who insisted the elusive beasts went the way of the unicorn. I've communicated with people in Spanish, Parisian French, and German, although I don't speak a word of those languages.

I've dialed a guest's cell phone number so she could find her cell phone in the mess that was her car's interior—but instead the covers on her bed began ringing. I've pulled all-nighters waiting for the lost, and taken a phone call at three in the morning from a broken-hearted teenager in desperate need of her mommy.

It's true, owning a bed-and-breakfast is hard work, but it also means I get to live in the mountains and the world comes to me. That's worth every monkey, every wrench.

People Who Need People

I found the cheapest gas station to fill my car's tank—and so did she. She was an old lady, and after pulling in behind my vehicle at the Mobil station at the corner of Broadway and State Street in Bangor, she cracked her car door just enough to allow her voice to be carried on air and waved me over.

"Is this one of those places you have to do this yourself?"

Yes, I thought, *unless you can get someone else to do it for you.*

To her I said, "Would you like me to do it for you?"

"Would you be a dear?" she pleaded and explained, "I have pneumonia and asthma." She was holding her gloved hand over her mouth as she talked, to prevent breathing in the cold January air. "And I coughed the entire month of December!"

I filled her tank. She was so appreciative. She dug around in the grocery bag on the passenger seat and tried to pay me in pudding.

That Time I Bought
a Snow Thrower

The bed-and-breakfast required a lot of love and attention, both inside and out. In the Maine mountains, outside love and attention also means cleaning up after a snowstorm.

After receiving and removing twenty-four inches of the white stuff on Valentine's Day, I didn't think my heart could stand moving another shovelful. So, I drove to the hardware store in Kingfield and did what any girl does when faced with a broken heart, I bought myself a big red Valentine—a snow thrower.

Chuck and Kevin, two local men who eventually became my very dear platonic friends, often stopped in to check on me, especially if I was standing in the yard in front of a new piece of equipment. On this particular day, one of them stopped to inspect my newest toy, and thought it best to quiz me on my knowledge of this new contraption.

"What's that black rubber contraption attached to the front?" he asked, pointing to a black rubber contraption strapped to the front.

"I have no idea," I admitted.

"What are these extra pegs for?" he said, pointing to two gold pegs.

"I'm not sure," I said, shrugging.

He couldn't believe I had bought a snow thrower without asking any questions about it.

"But I did ask a question!" I defended myself.

"What did you ask?"

"I asked how much I owed them."

He looked pained.

"I need snow out of my way, and it's a snow thrower," I said. "I figured that was pretty much everything I needed to know."

"Have you read the directions?" he asked.

"Well," I told him, "I can see through the plastic bag that holds the owner's manual that this is a Troy-Bilt two-stage snow thrower, and I'm thinking the two stages are 'on' and 'off,' so why do I need to read the directions?"

Grumbling, he continued to quiz me about my purchase.

"Why did you decide on this particular model?"

"This model"—I did my best Vanna White imitation as I gestured to it—"was three hundred dollars cheaper than the next model." (I couldn't believe he would think I don't carefully consider my purchases!)

I've lived in Maine pretty much my whole adult life, so I don't know why I never learned how to use a snow thrower. Past fortune, I guess.

It took only a little while for me to remember to engage the blades, but it took two incidents of near suffocation to remember to turn the chute away from my face. I also learned there's no ergonomically correct way to use one of these things—it was the boss, and it jerked me around and dragged me wherever it wanted. Most of the time I looked like a snow cone on a vibrating exercise machine gone wild; I just held on for dear life and let it go. (I was impressed it could shoot a rock farther than the power washer can throw an incorrectly attached nozzle!)

The machine had seven forward speeds—speed one moved like a slug stuck in mud and speed seven had me nearly horizontal, my feet slipping and sliding under me as I tried to keep up. The two reverse speeds were as slow as a spring thaw, and my impatience rose as rapidly as Stratton Brook does when ice jams under the bridge. So in haste I would pull back on it until my back gave out, and then I was once again suffering from a sore back—not from shoveling snow, but from throwing it.

I don't generally like mechanical guy things because usually that means they have moving parts that get me in trouble or cause me pain or both, but starting this new toy was a cinch. I just yanked on the cord and it started. Stopping it, however, proved to be more of a challenge. I thought about waiting for it to run out of gas, but a handy little note painted on the control panel suggested a cheaper modus operandi: "To Stop Engine, Move Throttle to Stop Position."

I called that same dear friend and asked him, "What's a throttle?" and received a colorful explanation from the other end of the line—in between expletives he managed to say, "read the manual!"

Still, I must have been doing something right, because the truckers driving by honked and waved. Could be my icicle dreadlocks, could be the comic relief, could be they were downright impressed and wanted to hire me.

This Old House?
She Owns Me.

She started her predawn grumbling around four o'clock on this deeply cold winter morning. At first she politely creaked, but I had become used to that, so I rolled over and went back to sleep. She then banged loudly enough to make me fully awake and aware that she wanted attention. Her objective is to wake me up, so I will warm her up by feeding the household fires. She is old and cold, cranky and complaining, unwilling to wait any longer. It seems that it is all about her, and as I dragged myself out of bed, I found myself wondering if it's time for me to give her up and move on. She is a fortress that demands my time, money, and fortitude. But like any lady, she is worth it. And besides, she is something I've always wanted—an old farmhouse in the mountains. I have come to believe that in calling myself her owner, the joke is on me. The truth is, it is quite the other way around. Because this is where I belong—she owns me.

She has been around for more than one hundred years and has passed the test of time. Even after all the interior changes made by those who lived here before—walls torn down, new walls added, new paint, rooms refurbished and a new roof built—her foundation never really changed. Her lines have settled in pleasant places, and

34

she stands where she always stood because that is what she is meant to do. She was what she was meant to be: a sturdy home alongside an ever-changing brook in an inevitably ever-changing little town.

Families of old were born here, grew up here, and then left her. She didn't mind, really. She recognized that is the way of life. New families would always replace the old, and they would also walk her antique oak floors, as they passed the new portraits hung on her walls.

I wonder if she has a favorite family. Was it the one with five boys or the one with three girls? I somehow doubt she favors individuals. I believe she is happy so long as there is contentment within the hearts of those who reside within her walls.

She has sheltered many. She has been a safe haven for the fledgling, a refuge to the homeless, and a comfort to the weary traveler. She is the birthplace of solid friendships, and along the way has weathered rain inside and out. She is full of all those things that make a life full.

I guess I'll keep her.

The front porch and door of Diamond Corner..

Six Degrees Below Zero

It was six degrees below zero this morning, and my washing machine drain froze. Unfortunately, I found this out by using it. After the rinse cycle, the water, unable to get past the ice jam, flooded the laundry room floor, then ran down the walls into my office beneath the laundry room. The water ruined my newly painted wall and the Vinology wine-making kit I've stored in the corner for the past five years. Maybe the wine isn't completely ruined, but I bet the Zinfandel, should I ever get around to making it, will have hints of Tide.

Cooking Lessons

I am a good cook. I'd say I was a great cook, but it took me forty years to become a good cook, so I don't expect to reach greatness until I'm well done—with life, that is.

I found a great-looking recipe for Warm Brown Rice Salad. It called for long grain brown rice and petite peas. Those sounded delicious, but the ingredients that caught my eye were champagne vinegar, two types of olive oil, Dijon mustard, basil, and parsley. I was instructed to combine the oils, vinegar, mustard, basil, and parsley in a mixing bowl. Using a wooden spoon, I stirred until my arm burned, but one driblet of mustard refused to become part of the whole and floated on the top in subversive separatism.

There was this thing on my counter, this whirligig-type of mechanical mixing thing that had been sitting there since Christmas, daring me to use it, so I did. As a result, my favorite pink T-shirt was sporting champagne vinegar, two types of olive oil, basil, parsley, and a driblet of Dijon mustard.

The garbage can was sporting a whirligig mechanical thing.

Until I owned a bed-and-breakfast, I didn't need to bake. I always had my grandmother to feed my sweet tooth and my babies, and we often indulged in the fruits of her labor. But now, with guests to feed and no grandmother's baking talents to feed upon, I was on my own. I searched for and found a recipe for coffee squares; the main ingredients being coffee and chocolate—two of God's perfect foods! I dutifully added all the ingredients, including one cup of instant coffee, which used up the better part of the jar.

It took nearly a week of soaking the pan in water to get the squares out. My mistake? The recipe called for one cup of brewed coffee, not one cup of instant coffee granules. That was an eye-opening experience.

One time I made chili, and a breeze coming through the open kitchen window turned the pages of my recipe book. Clam chowder with beans, anyone?

I made the most delicious chicken soup and, to go with it, a sweet, moist cornbread. The directions to the cornbread recipe said to remove the cooked bread from the pan immediately after taking it out of the oven. I turned the pan upside down over a cooling rack, only to have it defy the law of gravity. I wiggled a spatula under the cornbread all the way around the pan as far as I could and turned it over the rack again and slapped the bottom. The cornbread came out beautifully this time, not onto the cooling rack, but a little left of it, into a sink full of soapy dishwater.

Another time, I was whipping an egg white into a nice foamy consistency with my favorite whisk. I tipped the bowl a bit and all the nice foamy whipped egg slid to the side of the bowl, revealing a nightmarish sight—a finger in the bottom of the bowl! I screamed. The whisk and the eggs went flying. That's about when I realized the finger was mine—clearly visible through the bottom of the clear glass bowl.

I guess this boils down to one fact—in the kitchen, I'm about as thick as cold pea soup.

Don't Be Dead in Winter

The original Roman calendar had only ten months—March through December. It wasn't until 700 BC that January and February earned their names. January is named for Janus, the Roman God of Gates. Janus presided over doors and beginnings and is said to have two faces, one looking backward and the other looking forward. February is named for the Roman festival day of purification. I'll take that thought further—February air is pure.

Previously, January and February were not named because nothing was growing agriculturally. That seems a bit unfair to me, not to mention unimaginative. It's true that during the dead of winter there isn't much happening under the ground, but the land above is fully alive! It's a sparkling, crystal clear playground. This is the time of year for sleigh rides, snowmen, snowball fights, snowmobiling, cross-country or downhill skiing, snowshoeing, and ice fishing. It's the time of year to build castles—snow castles!

If none of those activities appeal to you, then just go for a walk and breathe in the fresh, frozen air. I promise it's worth it. I love the sound of snow crunching under my feet. There is nothing prettier than a field covered in white. The smooth blanket of snow covers the chaos of the forest floor. It's the best time of year to plainly see the tracks of critters.

Make January a new beginning on your personal calendar. Don't be dead in winter; get outside and play. Go out and live. "It's too cold!" you say? Remember, there really isn't any bad weather, only inappropriate clothing.

Rich Man, Poor Man

Here is a story of two Maine men—one rich, one poor—and a link between the two.

Ernest Linwood Dean and James Gregan were hardworking, intelligent men, but they lived on opposite sides of every social and economic scale that measures a town.

E. L. Dean, as he was known, was a savvy businessman who began climbing the ladder of opportunity at an early age. The first rung was working in the budding timber-harvesting industry in the early 1900s. Dean would climb the ladder further by working at the Hollingsworth and Whitney Company (which later became Scott Paper) and then set himself up for a life of financial freedom by using those profits to invest in Maine railroads. He owned an E. L. Dean Hardware Store and valuable property, and was a representative under Governor Charles Barrows. Civic minded, he served as a selectman and sat on nearly every board in town, including the hospital, the school, and the library. He was well known and powerful.

James Gregan was a humble, soft-spoken man who lived by the work of his hands. He could neither read nor write. Because I have seen his work, I believe this lack of worldly education allowed his God-given talent to fill that vacancy to overflowing. The boards on which he served were those under his gifted hands in his workshop. He was often paid for his services by nonmonetary means. On one such occasion his son was sent to collect a debt and returned home not with cash but a kerosene lamp. James Gregan worked for those who could pay only in barter, but also for the town elite, who hired him to build such homes as Greenville's esteemed Oak Hill mansion, commissioned in 1938 by Louis Oakes as a wedding gift to his daughter. Oakes became rich by investing money—including a two-thousand-dollar loan from E. L. Dean—in his brother Harry Oakes's gold mine in Kirkland, Ontario. Oak Hill is a twenty-room brick-and-timber Tudor-style mansion, now used as a luxury bed-and-breakfast. James Gregan was the head carpenter. That's a link, but a stronger one came much later.

Both were men of Greenville. One lived in a mansion, the other lived in a humble home on the other side of town, on the other side of the tracks.

Both Ernest Dean and James Gregan's children attended the small-town high school where classes were not separated, and because love can transcend everything, including railroad tracks, Dean's daughter and Gregan's son fell in love, married, stayed married for more than fifty years, and raised a family. Because of this, these two vastly different men would eventually become the very same thing—my great-grandfathers.

Because that's how life is in a small Maine town.

We Took to the Woods

The plan was as it always is when I visit my daughter, Kelly, and my grandson, Aiden—I drive him to school. Only this time, it was bird season, so we decided to leave a little early and stalk a few (to hopefully stock a few).

The woodland roads around Orrington, where he lives, are different from those in Stratton, where I live, mostly because the they have houses on them—lots of houses. We decided to go off road, and we turned onto an ATV trail and inched our way deep into the woods.

Our "heater hunting" (hunting while driving around with the car heat on) was going along fine until the Jeep sputtered, coughed, and died. I turned the key. The motor ticked at me. I turned the key again (just to be sure). Still nothing but an aggravating tick, tick, tick. We were stranded, and only heaven knew where.

My first thought was, "Don't panic."

My second thought was, "Oh, crap; I'm still in my pajamas."

After staring into space for the appropriate amount of time, so Aiden would believe I was devising a plan, I said, "Well, Grandson, I think we have to walk."

Aiden and I looked at each other for a long moment, and when no plan formed in his mind either, he said, "Guess so."

I sighed and pointed out, "I'm wearing my pajamas." Aiden gave me the once-over. It was then his turn to sigh, only he closed his eyes and shook his head as he did so.

Now, it's not unusual during hunting season in Maine to see a young man dressed in hunter orange walking along the side of the road with a shotgun under his arm. It is unusual is to see a pajama-clad grandmother, hugging herself against the cold, her huge old-lady purse slung over her shoulder, trudging along behind him. Aiden walked as if nothing was out of the ordinary. He has learned to take our outings in stride.

While we were traipsing along, I decided to point out all the silver linings: "This is not as bad as the time we got lost in the woods in Coplin Township and had to hike up that hill to find the lumber mill's smokestack so we would know the direction home," I said.

"And it's not as awful as the time we were bird hunting up by Elephant Mountain near Greenville and we lost track of time and were late getting back. Remember how mad your mother was? She grounded us from seeing each other for a whole month!

"And it's definitely not as bad as the time we lost the Jeep and had to walk home without it.

"And it's certainly not as traumatic as that time we learned our compass can tell us how to get from point A to point B but lacks the ability to tell us there is a two-mile-wide swamp in the middle.

"And it's not nearly as challenging as the time we were on that path of three-foot-deep mud and it sucked your boots off your feet.

"And how about that time the moose flies swarmed us and we had to jump into the freezing waters of the South Branch of the Dead River? That was much worse, wouldn't you agree?"

Aiden continued to walk ahead of me in silence.

As a last-ditch effort, I added, "At least this time it's daylight."

We walked for several more moments before Aiden finally voiced his opinion.

"Wow, Grandmother, we're pretty unlucky."

"At hunting or life in general?" I moaned.

He shrugged and I let it go at that; I didn't really want to know.

"You know, you might miss this morning's English class," I offered.

That encouraged him, and his steps slowed.

We finally reached pavement and waved down a guy backing out of his driveway. He cautiously cracked his window and peered suspiciously at us. I was prepared to tell him, "We don't expect you to let us into your car; we know how we look."

But I decided to keep the rest of my day simple and merely asked, "Would you kindly tell me the name of this road?"

Although his expression betrayed his curiosity, he did not ask for an explanation and I didn't offer one—life is sometimes simpler that way.

The end of this story isn't nearly as exciting as the beginning (or as exciting as it could have been had things gone further downhill), because once we learned where we were, we were no longer lost, and called for help that soon arrived. Eventually, Aiden made it to school and I made it home.

Best of all, the Jeep has a new alternator—and just in time for next week's deer hunting trip.

A Bear in the Basin

Aiden and I were skiing at Sugarloaf ski resort, in the gladed terrain of Brackett Basin. Although our love of skiing keeps us close, we sometimes lose sight of each other when skiing in the trees. That is exactly what happened on this particular adventure—I lost him. One moment he was beside me, but the next, I was alone in two-hundred-seventy acres of trees in a world of white and silence.

I skied down to two young men who were taking a break from their journey. They were sitting under a spruce, smoking pot, and drinking beer.

"Excuse me," I interrupted. "I seem to have lost my grandson. I don't suppose you've seen anyone ski past, have you?"

Their thoughts showed clearly through their clouded eyes. They couldn't believe I would bring a child into the glade and then lose him.

All of a sudden, a giant black thing—my mind instantly imagined it was a huge bear—flew over the cliff above me and landed with a loud thud behind me. The snow around the thing exploded into the air, creating a mini-blizzard. Sticks and skis and bits and pieces of things catapulted skyward. Growling was heard. Then laughter.

Pure, joy-filled laughter.

I turned and looked at the bear-bomb. I turned back to the tree dwellers and said, "Never mind; there he is."

My grandson, Aiden, looking out at a deer in the backyard.

Don't Feed the Donkeys

Deer regularly passed through the backyard of the bed-and-breakfast, and although I understand it is controversial to feed them, I did. The deer would bed down on the island in Stratton Brook for safety, then "yard up" across the road in the woods, which means their path each morning crossed my backyard, or I should say my backyard was in their path because they were here first. I figured I might as well feed them while I was feeding the guests.

The guests enjoyed watching the deer through the dining-room patio doors, and many mornings I had to remind them to sit down before their breakfast got cold.

A child from Connecticut who had never seen a deer before, other than those in movies or pictures, came barreling down the stairs, yelling, "There's a donkey in the backyard!"

Another guest, seeing deer out the window while he was in the second-story bathroom did the same, only in his excitement, he yelled, "There's a deer in the bathroom upstairs!"

I had guests with children who had never seen so much snow. Maine gave them quite the education with a classic Nor'easter. An eight-year-old boy was amazed that the snow made our sidewalks indistinguishable from our streets. He and his ten-year-old sister built three snowmen in the backyard and made snow angels for the first time in their lives. They made so many, the backyard looked like heaven.

Their mother wanted to leave an hour early to drive four miles up the road to the Porter House Restaurant. She wanted to make sure they were on time for their reservation. I could almost understand that, but I nearly left the kitchen in a fit of laughter when she tried to explain to her son what a snowmobile is: "It's sort of a motorcycle," she said, "but bigger!" Except, I then remembered a Southern belle friend I had in South Carolina. She had never seen snow and thought a Ski-Doo was the name of a horse, reminding me we don't know things we don't know until we know them.

The Ride to Abraham

The map was hastily drawn on a cocktail napkin, a series of intersecting lines symbolizing trails and a few warped circles representing landmark boulders. Our mode of transportation—snowmobiles. Our destination—the top of Mount Abraham. We nearly made it, too.

The men in the group wondered from the start whether my sled could make the final, steep ascent. Their true worries were finding the right route to the top of this mountain within the maze of unmarked backcountry trails, and, once we reached the summit, whether we would get back home in time for the green flag of the day's NASCAR race. We were having difficulty on this, our first attempt at Abraham, and when one of the guys pulled the map out of his pocket for the umpteenth time, I started to eyeball things in a whole new light, for I drank an entire thermos of coffee and forgot to pack toilet tissue.

I left the burden of the search to my sledding partners, who huddled over a malfunctioning GPS and smudged cocktail napkin, while I took pictures of the surrounding mountains—Saddleback to the southwest, Sugarloaf to the northeast, and our goal, the peak of Abraham, teasing us with her nearness. During that time three things developed—two of the pictures and my awareness of our insignificance in the universe. Thousands of acres of wilderness lay before me, and in the vastness, I felt as microscopic as a crystal in a snowflake and as invisible as the water vapor that forms them.

We rode through several new plantings of spruce and fir. I found the older, taller hardwoods comical, their sun-bleached, bare branches towering over the younger stands. They reminded me of schoolchildren in a packed classroom, the taller trees being those whiz kids who, knowing the answer, stand with raised arms and branched fingers in intense anticipation of being called on.

"Oh, oh, teacher, teacher, me, me, call on me . . ."

Remember those kids? They have been petrified in wood up here.

The wind was high, and several rocky peaks were becoming bare because of it. As I watched, gusts of wind took the form of snow-blown ghosts, complete with heads and swirling arms that reached for the craggy mountaintops in an attempt to grab hold and settle. But the wind had her way, and her turbulent mood sent the squalls into the air, where they vanished.

We eventually found the trail to the top, but did not summit. On the final leg we met a slope of ice and a guardian angel in the form of a white-haired guy from Winterport who noticed one of the sleds in our group was about to lose its front ski. A bolt was missing, and the main screw that held the ski to the sled was free and about to become even freer.

So, while our guys, the guy from Winterport, and his buddy (whom I stared at while I tried to decide if he was a she or a he, until he finally removed his helmet and hat and was introduced to us as Willard) attended to the loose ski dilemma, I attended to a block of pepper jack cheese, a tube of summer salami, and a thermos of blueberry wine.

We were up there, nearly at the top of Abraham, long enough for me to learn that the wife of the guy from Winterport was celebrating a birthday the next day, but not so long that I learned the his name, probably because that information surfaced while I was focusing on finding out if Willard was a woman. We turned around less than a quarter mile from the top, not disappointed, for we enjoyed the day, met new friends, and admired the splendor of the wilderness. After all, the mountain will always be there, although the same is not true for us.

That day we lived a truism: the thrill is not always in the arrival, but in the ride.

It's All Relatives

Greenville is where my family is from, where my parents and my grandparents grew up—our hometown. Not only does everyone here know each other, we're all related to one another. (That's why we learned at a young age never to say anything bad about anybody—we never knew if we were bad-mouthing a family member.)

One morning at my sister's restaurant, Auntie M's, I had a conversation with a couple from Virginia. They had a lot of questions, the first being about the weather. She thought it was cold.

"It's forty-three degrees outside; that's not cold, that's refreshing," I educated her. "Cold is when it's forty-three degrees below zero."

She shivered.

Her second question was where to buy food and wine. I told them they could go to the local grocer up the hill, but they should buy their wine at a smaller market across town.

"Because they have a good selection of wine?"

"Well, yes, of course," I said, "but mostly because my brother-in-law owns it."

Then I added a riddle. "His wife owns this business."

The gentleman looked confused, but only for a moment as his wife was quick to explain, "His wife is her sister," she said.

He nodded and we moved on.

"And the grocery store on the hill isn't local?" she wanted to know.

"Yes, it is a hometown business," I clarified. "Truth be known, their niece is also my niece, but on the other side of the aisle. You see, this town is so tight-knit even the relatives who aren't relatives are related."

They had to think about that one for a bit, then chuckled.

The conversation turned to lodging. He told me they were renting from an owner-based rental business.

"The next time you visit," I suggested, "you should contact the rental company here. My cousin owns it. Well, she did. She recently sold it to a national company, but my daughter still works there."

The two of them were shaking their heads at this point. He wanted to know what other businesses in town were family.

My mind wandered up and down the streets as I listed, "The pharmacy, the gift shop on the corner, the sportsman shop (we share a grandchild), the girl at the bank, another one at the town office, a few of the teachers, the electrician, the owner of the child-care center, the massage therapist, the real estate agent, a couple of local band members."

I took a breath before continuing.

"We don't have any doctors or lawyers in the family," I said. "But the guy who does the town's firewood is related, and that's just as handy."

Hearing myself, I had to admit this sounded unbelievable, even to me, except it's true. Because that is what Maine towns are built on—families.

As the couple left the restaurant, they picked up a copy of my book *Maine Stories* on display for sale by the door. (My sister graciously allows me to sell them at her business.) As they paid for it, they jokingly asked me if the author was related to me, since it seemed to them that everyone else in town was.

"Let me just say," I answered, "I know her well."

Not Enough Time

Our winter world may seem dormant, but for an owner of a bed-and-breakfast that is close to two ski areas and thousands of miles of snowmobiling and cross-country ski trails, winter around here is anything but latent. It is the time of year I am the busiest! I have more to do than time in which to do it.

I thought perhaps a to-do list might help me get organized enough to be productive. I jotted it down.

1. Don't panic.
2. Eat.
3. Email my friends to tell them how much I have to do.
4. Call my mother and tell her how much I have to do.
5. Put all the piles—newspapers, bills, clothing, books, etc.—in neat stacks so they look not so not neat.
6. Alphabetize the spices.
7. Pick off the wax that dripped down the side of the candle in the bathroom.
8. Realize that 6 and 7 are coping mechanisms, namely denial, and scratch them off the list.
9. Stop stalking people on Facebook.
10. Do an hour of yoga to encourage my focusing skills.
11. Make out the Christmas list for my daughters.

My Christmas list:

Holland: Nothing because she graduated from high school, moved into her own place, went to work, and didn't stay home to help me.

Emily: Nothing because she went to college and didn't stay home to help me.

Kelly: Nothing because I can't play favorites.

Meeting the Guests

Guests at my B&B are all unique, each one is different from the rest, and all stay for just a little while. I only get to see them up-close if I take the time.

Mostly, I only get a glimpse.

It was six thirty in the morning. Ryan the Adorable (as I call him) had just left. He was here from Methodist College in Fayetteville, North Carolina, where he was, as I understood it, studying golf. I didn't know there was a golf school for Methodists. Imagine. Ryan's tee time was seven at Sugarloaf, so I sent him off with a breakfast sandwich of two slices of pumpkin bread held together with my "Out Back" raspberry jam.

The guest staying in the room "Weeds" went to Cornell University. He was a good-looking, highly intelligent young man. He worked in downtown New York City in the high finance district, doing global stuff, you know. He had an apartment overlooking Central Park. He knew lots of stuff about lots of stuff. One thing he obviously didn't know about was the featherbed toppers we use on our beds. He evidently thinks they are extra big comforters because he slept *under* his. Made me feel darn right smart.

We had the nicest couple here from Vinalhaven. They were using a B&B gift certificate given to them by their fellow teachers before they moved to Colorado, where they were going to earn their master's degrees. They brought their canary, Isabella.

Holland and I fell in love with Isabella, but even though they couldn't take her out west, they wouldn't let us have her. He didn't want to tell us why.

We finally wheedled it out of him.

He sheepishly admitted, "We are stopping at my mother's on our way to Colorado. She wants Isabella because it's her grand-bird."

One guest was an optometrist who could do the weirdest things with her eyeballs! They pretty much move independently of one another. She said that was the "thing to do" in optometry school: learn how to do strange eyeball maneuvers.

Elfrieda, an Austrian, was a used-parts salesperson, only instead of the car-part salesman that that description conjures up, she found, bought, and resold technology to foreign businesses—a word processing chip to Italy, a modem to Madrid, that sort of thing. Researching her potential customers was a large part of her home-based business. On more than one occasion, after investigating certain groups, she found them to have questionable motives. Therefore she denied them the parts they requested. A technology that could register how far "out there" my imagination traveled has yet to be invented.

Paula was a lovely lady from England who talked with the most charming accent. She was quite interested in my business and my guests. She wanted to know when more were arriving and why they were coming to the area.

"The next guests are arriving on Thursday for the regional AA conference being held at Sugarloaf," I told her. "There are more than a thousand reformed alcoholics expected."

With a shocked expression and in her very prim and proper British accent she asked, "What in heaven's name does one do if one can't have a drink in the evening?"

"I guess I'll have to ask Thursday's guests," I told her.

We hosted a radiology oncologist from South Africa who immigrated to Kingston, Ontario. He, his wife Elsabe (I love that name!), and their little daughter Esther had a distinct accent, which exuded a genteel formality. They said things like "terribly so" and used words such as "shall" and "lovely."

Three-year-old Esther, upon discovering Holland's seven-room, fully furnished dollhouse, declared to her parents in a little doll voice

The living room at Diamond Corner, featuring the seven-room dollhouse.

and stately manner, 'I shall stay here and you may pick me up on your return." She then turned to me and politely requested a stool so she could reach the object of her desire and cause of her desertion.

After meeting all these people and noticing their idiosyncrasies, I thought: This is the wonderful thing about us, this is the thing that makes us different from all other species—our uniqueness, our individualism, our wackiness. Some of us talk too much; some of us don't talk enough. Some of us ride snowmobiles; some of us ride horses. Some of us are amazed by snow; some of us are amazed by nothing. But all of us deserve to be listened to, even if we talk with an accent or if we talk too fast or if we aren't understood. We can all learn something if we listen.

Another guest, an Asian clothing designer named Milui, was as wiry as thread. Her tiny size and the huge amount of food she consumed made me think her styles were still waiting to come into fashion.

Joni was the only B&B guest from America that was out of my realm. She was a middle-aged woman who decided to change her career from counselor to joyologist. She wanted to make a living spreading joy (joy the state of mind, not Joy the dish detergent). I believe cleaning the crud out of your life goes a long way toward finding joy, but I'm not convinced joy is something you can get just by someone spreading it on you. Joni was here with her friend Dean, a perfusionist at a large hospital. A perfusionist is the person in charge of artificially replacing the circulatory or respiratory functions of a patient undergoing open heart surgery. I immediately identified the possible collaboration in Dean and Joni's professions, but Dean didn't think Joni should be adding stuff to someone's heart that wasn't there before surgery. He didn't want his patients' hearts bubbling over with anything just after an operation; it might make their recovery a bit too lively.

It's a Wonder
Any of Us are Alive

Perhaps it was because of Presidents' Day. Maybe it was because I'm a history buff (especially American history and personal family history.) Whatever the reason, I was recently reading about Abraham Lincoln and my ancestry—not that the two are related.

I enjoy the personal stories I discover. Like finding out my Scottish great-great-great-great-great-grandfather was friends with the poet Robert Burns. This means nothing now, of course; it's just interesting. I don't even like the poems of Robert Burns. That's my shortcoming, for sure. It's undoubtedly because Burns wrote in the Scottish dialect of the 1780s, and I understand only about every fifth word.

Another fascinating discovery was learning there is gold buried on the family farm. They say that my great-great-grandfather buried his gold on his farm in Kouchibouguac, New Brunswick, but he never told anyone where it was. While he lay dying in bed, he attempted to tell people something important, but they were unable to make out his words. They believe he was trying to tell them where he buried his treasure. Can you imagine the look on their faces when he breathed his last breath, and they realized the secret stayed just that?

My most fascinating discovery was learning how close I came to not being. During my recent trip to the past, I discovered Abraham Lincoln, one of our country's best loved and greatest men, does not have any direct descendants. Three out of four of Abe's children died in childhood, and his family line ended in 1985 when his childless great-grandson died. That is very similar to my family history. All six children of my great-great-great-grandparents died, most in childhood, from various diseases—the only saving grace being that one who lived long enough to bear a child before she died of tuberculosis at the age of thirty. My family very narrowly escaped going the way of Lincoln's. Given the almost incomprehensible span of time—the years, the decades, the centuries, the milleniums—it was one fragile yet successful nine-month gestation period, a mere nine months of health out of all that time, is the reason I'm alive. Also, taking into consideration the incidence of disease, and human frailty, it's a wonder that any of us are alive. This makes me pause and realize it's a miracle I'm sitting here writing this story. Do you understand what a miracle it is that you're sitting there reading it?

You Need Scissor Skills

My daughter Holland was never much of a student; she couldn't help it, it was her legacy. I was called into the principal's office because of her nearly as often as I sat there because of myself, back when it was me who wasn't much of a student.

The first time I sat across from a cross teacher was when Holland was in kindergarten. Mrs. March offered me a child-sized chair. When I sat with my chin nearly touching my knees and she sat opposite me in her adult-sized chair, it was obvious something was amiss.

"Is everything all right?" I asked.

"Not really," Mrs. March said. "We have a problem; Holland lacks scissor skills."

"She what?" I leaned in to hear her more clearly.

"She. Lacks. Scissor. Skills," Mrs. March slowly pronounced each syllable so I could better understand her.

"She's five!"

My lower jaw bumped my knees.

"Holland needs to master scissor skills in order to be promoted to first grade," the teacher explained.

Mrs. March was as serious as a paper cut when she presented me with a pair of mutant scissors with four finger holes—not the usual two—so I could put my hand around my child's hand and

My youngest daughter, Holland.

help her learn how to cut stuff out. My eyes were as round as the finger holes in Mrs. March's teaching scissors.

"It's a small-muscle development skill," she said.

I felt a small muscle in my cheek develop a tic.

"Judy," I said. (The absurdity of the situation called for the seriousness of using her first name.) "If Holland still can't use scissors by the time she graduates from high school we will worry then, okay?"

On her very first report card Holland earned a minus next to "controls scissors well," which I thought was the unkindest cut of all because you see, I understood. Like Holland, I couldn't control my scissors either. As hard as I tried, my cuts always produced ragged edges. (I still have ragged edges.)

I clearly remember the day in third grade when my teacher tried to teach me how to make my rough edges smooth like everyone else's. I struggled, but failed. It wouldn't be until many years and countless lessons later that I would learn how to cut things out literally and figuratively in my life. The first thing to go was the idea that I had to be like everyone else. The second thing was that I had to conform to the world. I eventually learned to snip those things that don't improve my life— jealousy and spitefulness, regret and bitterness, love of money, love of self, disrespect, and discontent. I whittle my life with a blade honed on a stone made of a good memory of bad decisions.

Holland, you are a senior about to graduate from high school, you are ready to embark on your future. The world that lies before you is full of beautiful things, interesting people, exciting adventures, love, and happiness. It is also brimming with mediocrity, cruelty, ugliness, and evil. For the remainder of your life all the decisions and choices that need to be made for you will be made by you. My prayer is that you cut out those things that do harm. To that end, Holland, my dear little girl, Mrs. March was right. You need scissor skills.

SPRING

It Must Be Spring

I could tell it was spring because the toe of my slipper had just blown out. One stitch let go, and the rest followed like undisciplined little snots. Slipper failure is always a sign that winter is nearing its end.

I love spring.

A messy yard is another sign of spring, and mine was a perfect example. With the melting snow, all the regular nasty spring stuff—like mud and dog poop—began showing up, but also emerging was stuff that fell out of my daughter Holland's car every time she opened the door during the winter. One day I found a pair of her socks in the driveway, still partially covered with snow. They'd obviously been there a while. It seemed as if someone else noticed them, too, and tried to pick one up, but, because the heel remained frozen in the ground, the sock ripped. Whoever tried to retrieve it had no choice but to leave it there, beside its mate. That one remained undisturbed and whole, the toe seam frozen in a triumphant smile.

Closer to where I park, I saw a receipt under the ice. There was not the slightest wrinkle to mar the print, and I could read every item on it. Not until the thaw would I be able to get my hands on it and destroy the evidence that I paid way too much for a pair of shoes.

The Christmas tree that did not make it to the dump, but instead was dumped in the yard, became visible again, as did three dog bones (one crushed into a thousand pieces by a vehicle), a blue stuffed animal, a Dunkin' Donuts cup, something lime green, and several pieces of tar paper that blew off the roof. It was little wonder the crocuses and snowdrops hadn't surfaced—they would be humiliated.

Of all the bizarre things coming into sight, the strangest was some moose parts (I'm not making this up.) Out front, under the town Christmas tree, a moose jaw poked out of a melting snowbank. I didn't see the rest of him, so I have to believe the rest of him was never there. His jaw must have dropped off the back of a truck after last fall's hunting season.

Since it didn't seem as if Stratton Brook was going to flood my yard this year and wash away all the winter debris, I knew I needed to rake it all up, and I did—once the rake became visible.

Guests Who Make You Go "Hmmmm"

Because I live a life on the periphery of guests' lives, I do not delve into the details of their lives. For example, one lady showed up a day late and upon entering the house said, "I would have been here yesterday, but my son had his court date."

There was a woman who had such an allergy to meat that she couldn't eat anything cooked in my oven because meat had been cooked in there at one time or another. Her mother was nice enough, though, and cut up her daughter's pancakes because the daughter complained that her shoulder hurt from driving—all the way from New Hampshire.

There was the man who couldn't find his room, even though there were only four of them and they were all on the same floor. He stood in the hall late that evening, calling out to his wife, "Linda! Linda!"

Linda opened their bedroom door and said, "Jesus, Fred! You're an idiot!"

I could hear muffled laughter from behind the other guest room doors.

There was a pothead groupie who pointed to my snowmobile in the yard and asked, "How fast does that chicken go?"

There was an Appalachian Trail thru-hiker who decided to stay a couple of extra days because she got hooked on the World Poker Championship on ESPN and needed to watch the outcome. One afternoon she sat on the living room couch, clothed only in a towel while her hiking partner did their laundry at the local laundromat (obviously every single piece of it). Just so you know, all the rooms had their own TVs.

There was the guy who got into an argument with a fellow group member just before they arrived and he stayed in his room the entire weekend. I asked the leader of the group if that man was alright. Her answer included a shrug. "He's different." On the morning of his departure, he disappeared before the moon did.

There was a man who was so big, he broke the toilet seat. Another large guy wanted a partial refund because he couldn't sit in a kayak. It kept flipping over when he sat in it. I will forever regret not witnessing that.

There was a psychologist who claimed to truly hate people.

I had to smile at a guest who, instead of putting her empty cracker box into the wastebasket in her room, filled it with garbage instead. That is not so much the story as is her thought process as she stuffed the box full of gum wrappers, snack wrappers, and tissues. She must have thought she was saving one of two things—me from work or the world from another bag of garbage. Yes, that's it—the world has one less bag of garbage, but alas, has one more box of it.

I had a guest who explained at length the different coat shades that collie dogs have and the meaning of each. Her lecture included color photographs. While she educated us, her sister sat on the couch and compared a paint chip from her purse to the pictures in all my decorating magazines, which, being a big part of the B&B business, counts to quite a few.

Place Settings

By the time I was ten years old, my list of household chores included setting the table for our family of eight. This was back in the day when it was fashionable for families to eat dinner together, and being fashionable, we did.

I would hold the eight dinner plates in my left arm and, with an imagination powerful enough to turn those plates into a stack of corporate quarterly reports, I passed them out with my right hand to the imaginary board members sitting in the chairs around our dining room table.

"Here you go, Mr. Dobbs," and, "One for you, Mr. Pinkerton." I was all business as I placed the silverware, telling the people who were visible to my eye alone, "You will need a pencil, Ms. Joyce." As I placed a fork down at the next report, I said, "And a highlighter for you, Mr. Wood." I placed a knife: "Miss Rodenberry—your pen." And then, with all the executives outfitted with the proper papers and utensils, I skipped out of the room, returning to Miss Rodenberry's seat when dinner was served.

Although my mother may remember things differently, I do not remember complaining. I don't recall thinking anything odd about it being my chore, not my brother's, to set the table. I don't remember what his chore was—maybe it was to feed the dog or mow the lawn. Maybe it was to clean up after dinner. Maybe he didn't have chores. I don't remember. I don't remember what my three sisters were responsible for either, because that is not the point.

The point is, my job was to set a precise table. I was expected to do it to the best of my ability and correctly. I know how many forks to use, and I know which fork goes where. I know it is considered proper to serve from the right. Why do I know these things? Because I was properly raised.

Today, I am a businesswoman. I own my own business, a successful bed-and-breakfast, which puts me in the business of setting places around the breakfast table—again.

This is my place setting. Plates and circles.

Isn't it funny how life circles around?

I Can't Think of a Title, Either

I love being a writer, but there is a downside to it—I have to sit down and write. I must force myself to stop waiting to be inspired by the snowflakes on my window, the nuts in my granola, the nuts and flakes staying at my B&B, or the way avocados look, all green and bumpy. Instead of working, I play games—head games and computer games. My favorite is called FreeCell. It's a computer game, for if it were a game in my head, it would be called PrisonCell. FreeCell is absolutely amazing, and the odds are with me that I may actually beat the computer if I play four thousand more times today. I'll have to go for it, of course.

Instead of sitting down and getting down to the business of writing, I find myself alphabetizing the cereal collections and the canned vegetables. I repeatedly check the bird feeders to make sure they stay crammed full of seed just in case a cardinal wants to join the hundreds of chickadees that have found bird heaven—thanks to the wacko on the other side of the glass and her endless supply of sunflower seeds, cracked corn, and thistle seed.

Instead of working, I stare out the kitchen window, which isn't such a terrible thing until hour three comes and goes. The thing that should have alarmed me during that time was not when I told

Holland's golden retriever Sadie, "There goes a hot tub down the road," but when I explained to her, "I don't mean it went down the road alone, it was on a trailer behind a truck."

It's not that I didn't have anything about which to write—I have oodles of stuff to say. I could write about my friend who splits her own firewood. Miraculously, she has never chopped her leg or lost a toe. When I voiced my apprehension at the chance of doing just that, she explained the act of chopping is just like playing golf. The trick to keeping hold of your toes, she says, is to keep your eye on the target like you keep your eye on the golf ball. Since I don't play golf, I had absolutely no idea what she was talking about, so that column didn't survive the chopping block.

I could write about the four-year-old darling I met, a blondie after my own heart. When asked if she wanted an ice cream cone, she blinked her saucer-sized blue eyes and innocently asked, "Is it cold?"

I could tell about my most embarrassing moments, like the time I was driving along, singing with Celine Dion, but when I tried to hit the high note, I hyperventilated and had to pull over to recover. Although that is not the only embarrassing moment I have had, it is the only one I dare admit to, so that column idea is kaput.

It is now past noon, and I have not one word of my story written. Perhaps after I take the dog for a walk to see which one of the neighbors has a new hot tub, I'll think of something.

Nice, Grandmother.

We were warned. We can't say we weren't.

The ATV trail behind Claude's gas station had a sign: "Very deep mud hole, use alternate route."

So, I backed up my Honda 300 FourTrax and asked Claude about it. He said the hole had been there a long time and had actually become legendary. He said a lot of folks were getting stuck. "Burying their machines," were his exact words. He also explained it was illegal to take four-wheelers on the only alternate route—a paved road. "But it didn't rain yesterday or today. You never know, the mud hole could have dried up," he added.

My grandson Aiden and I were intrigued, and intrigue is a valid reason to go, just to have a looksee, you understand, not to attempt a crossing. I'm not stupid. We did just that and found mud holes like this one don't dry up; they grow and take on an evil life of their own.

Yup, the hole was huge, about as big as Pumpkin Pond and as dark as the finest Belgian chocolate. It was a forbidding chocolate lake with eyes. I swear I saw a sea monster (maybe that was a bullfrog).

We stopped on the edge of the abyss, and our two helmeted heads, one slightly taller than the other, shook slowly side to side with amazement as we gazed upon the mire.

"Nice," Aiden said.

"Yeah, nice," I echoed, and our eyes followed a lost sandal as it floated by. The edges of the mud hole, if there were any, must have been at least a dozen yards into the grasses on either side. Aiden, still not convinced I was a woman of discriminating judgment, gave me a doubt-filled, sidelong glance and asked, "We're not doing it, are we, Grandmother?"

"Of course not," I insisted, miffed by his doubt. "I'm just looking."

While we sat there on the edge, on my little machine, I had a strange sensation—a downward movement. The solid ground beneath us, in horror-movie-come-to-life action, turned into huge, hungry brown lips and sucked us in. The hole, having given us a chance to leave and seeing we did not take it, decided we were going to stay forever. We were stuck, sunk to our boots.

Now part of the legend.

Not a tree in sight to winch to.

Not a person in sight to hear me yell.

I dismounted and assessed the situation.

Aiden dismounted and assessed the situation.

He stood, arms akimbo, as he checked all four tires. The four-wheeler sank another inch, and the hole popped a gloating bubble. Aiden's eyebrow disappeared under his helmet as he glared at me.

"Nice, Grandmother," he said, disgusted.

I silently cursed all machines and mentally made a promise to myself from this moment on I would use the only faithful form of transportation—my legs. Then, the memory of the morning's stiff and painful stairway descent detoured that line of thinking.

"Grandson?"

"Yeah?" His eyebrow was still missing; his mood had not improved.

"We have to hike home and get the big ATV."

"So you can get that one stuck too, Grandmother?"

I shook my granny finger at his turned-up nose and warned, "Sassy pants carries the backpack."

"Nice, Grandmother," he mumbled under his breath.

I did not want to be seen walking downtown so soon after having been seen riding the ATV to the trailhead. That would be an admission of failure. It doesn't matter what kind of failure: mechanical failure, ran-into-a-tree failure, crossing failure, it's all failure. So, we took the long way home through the woods. I was surprised Aiden didn't complain. I thought his silence was, well, rather nice. (Honestly, I think he was too busy plotting against me to complain.) Perhaps the heaviness of the backpack was occupying his mind.

We powered up the Polaris 550 HO and headed back to the hole, through town, where we had just been seen on the smaller machine.

"Failure, huh?" said one person.

"Need help?" asked another.

"You'll get the hang of it," assured a third.

"Nice, Grandmother," Aiden said, appalled.

Using the bigger machine, we pulled the smaller stuck one out. Aiden figured that since we now had two machines, he would drive the Honda, and was aghast to learn the law was against him. He perceived it as a total betrayal of trust in his talents and was boisterously vocal on the issue.

"Oh, that's nice!" he protested.

We took the smaller machine home—muddy and untrustworthy as it was—and walked back through town, smiling at the curious stares we received, back to the hole to retrieve the Polaris for use for the remainder of the day.

On our ride to Rangeley we got chewed by blackflies, punctured by mosquitoes, lost once, stuck twice (but only once bad enough to need the winch), and whacked by tree branches six times, and with each calamity Aiden voiced his displeasure: "Nice, Grandmother!"

Once we reached our destination, Aiden, in outright mutiny, sat on the curb downtown and declared he had every intention of hitching a ride back to Stratton.

"You get on that machine right this minute, young man, or I'll bungee you to the rack!" I warned him.

"Nice. Way to threaten a little kid, Grandmother!"

He grudgingly climbed aboard, and the ride home was what it should be—dirty, muddy, sweaty, grit in your teeth, nice.

That night as I tucked Aiden into bed, the memories of the hole and the mishaps still fresh in my mind, I still dared to ask him, "How was your day, Grandson?"

He put his arms around my neck, kissed my cheek, and sleepily whispered in my ear, "Nice, Grandmother."

I Have Friends
Who Know Things

When I first started baking pies, I had three rhubarb plants in my garden—plants that had been there probably longer than I had been on the earth. I eventually turned those three plants into fifteen but until then, I had to buy rhubarb from a local farmer, especially in spring when everyone and their brother wanted strawberry rhubarb pies—except for one elderly gentleman who said, "My grandmother never would have put strawberries in her strawberry-rhubarb pie!"

No doubt prompted by the look on my face, he then educated me, "Strawberry rhubarb is a type of rhubarb." Who knew? We do now.

I've had a long experience with rhubarb. I remember going out to my great-grandmother's garden and grabbing a stalk of rhubarb and eating it. I loved the tart taste. Little did I know that this vegetable would grow to be such a big part of my adult life.

Now, I have friends who know things—secret things of the woods. Hidden things. Long-ago abandoned treasures. Things people need, crave, covet. I have friends who know where all the long-gone farms stood. Best of all, they know where to find the left-behind rhubarb plants.

They keep these plants a selfish secret.

I needed rhubarb to fill pie orders as my three plants were all used up. After enduring the most pathetic whining to ever torture the human ear, my friends shared their secret plant whereabouts (but not *their* rhubarb) with me. This was after they extracted a solemn promise of silence, which, if broken, could quite possibly end our friendship. Only then was I enlightened regarding the whereabouts of these treasures, these rhubarb plants.

"Turn right after the bridge and drive about two miles. At the fourth left, turn onto a dirt road. About a mile down that road on your right is a field. Walk to the far end of the field and toward the lilac bush."

The family is gone, the farmhouse is gone, even the foundation is hidden by a bramble of berry bushes, but the rhubarb plants live on. Oftentimes, a lilac tree in the woods is a hint, a good indication, of a former homestead. The original homesteaders brought lilacs with them from Europe and planted them near the entry to their house, or over the old outhouse hole when that building needed relocating, or, because the flower of the lilac is a symbol of innocence, purity, and lost love, over the grave of a loved one, especially an infant.

The secret directions continued: "That is where you'll find a nice-sized rhubarb plant. And don't forget—pull the stalk, don't cut it!" (Pulling the stalk separates it from the plant near the root and tells the plant to regrow a new stalk in its place. If you cut the stalk, no message is sent to the root and so, no new stalk.)

Always looking over my shoulders to see if I was being watched, I would sneak through the overgrown field to find the abandoned plant and be dismayed to see someone else had already found and harvested it. Thankfully, that didn't happen often because the rhubarb-secret sisters were terrified of each other and the secret was held close to heart.

I eventually researched how to propagate the three rhubarb plants that were in my backyard and grew them into fifteen more huge plants. During its season, the pulled rhubarb from my garden covered my kitchen counter as well as the table on my porch; it held open the pages of my recipe books and filled my fridge. It was in my face so much for so long, I can even spell it without looking it up—rhubarb.

The Yodeler

I stopped for breakfast at a restaurant in the small northern Maine town of Millinocket. The eatery was so obscure that I'm convinced the only reason I was there was that it found me. Have you heard the term a hole-in-the-wall? This place was the place inside the hole-in-the-wall. The red-checkered tablecloths clearly had been on the tables since 1950, and the tiles that lined the bar were chipped and faded. The laminated tables and plastic-covered chairs were so old, they were back in style.

Sitting at the end of the bar in this old diner was an old man. Harold was his name, and he was dressed in green work pants and a tan shirt. The elbows of his shirt were worn as thin as his body. His skinny legs were crossed, and his bony hands, at the end of scrawny arms, were cupped around a stained coffee cup. His face was deeply lined, and I guessed him to be more than eighty years old, although I learned he was not yet sixty. He had an innocence about him, and as he conversed with the waitress, it became clear to me that his mind, like his manner, was childlike.

I found out Harold was in the habit of walking down the streets of town, yodeling as he went. In response to my question, he admitted he taught himself to yodel simply because he liked the way it sounded. This intrigued me, so I asked him to sing. His face lit up. His eyes twinkled like a child who knows a secret. His features softened and he suddenly looked as young as his mind. He took a deep breath and yodeled, tapping his foot in perfect rhythm against the bar's brass footrest. A haunting hymn filled the room. It was a sweet, delicate sound that mingled with the aroma of brewed coffee and old wood, and kind souls who halted conversations to tilt their heads his way and listen. I have yet to hear a more charming sound than that of this simple-minded yodeler, or see a more heart-warming scene than the one in this humble little diner. The differences that compose all humanity vanished in the musical bars of the man at the bar as he closed his eyes and sang from his heart.

When he finished, the audience widened his smile with their applause. I complimented him on his gift, and the waitress chimed in to tell me, "Harold can also play the harmonica." Harold, in anticipation of another chance to perform, excitedly asked her if music was allowed in the diner. He didn't wait for her answer, but enthusiastically insisted, "You call me when music is allowed!" The waitress promised she would. She reached for a napkin and asked him for his phone number. Harold, with chin in fragile hand, frowned at his feet and for a long moment tried to remember. For him, the world of numbers proved more difficult than the world of music, and in the end, he was able to give her only his memorized address: "Ninety-three Pine."

He suddenly jumped off his stool as if his body had just caught up to the thought his mind had had several minutes earlier. As he headed toward the door, he repeated over and over, "Ninety-three Pine. Ninety-three Pine. When there is music, call me at Ninety-three Pine."

The waitress absentmindedly dried her hands on her apron as she watched the yodeler walk down the street, singing as he went. His song faded, then disappeared as he rounded a corner and did the same.

I heard her whisper to herself, "Harold, you are the music."

All Along the Dump Road

I get painful cramps in my neck, in my shoulders, and in my hands, but the most damaging cramps of all attack my brain—writer's cramps. To combat them I take long walks west on Route 16, which is just out my front door. My neighbor once asked me why I always take that route.

"Don't you tire of the same old scenery?" she asked.

"I live on the dump road; the scenery changes constantly," I replied.

For example, one day I found a brand-new old lady purse. It still had the price tag marked: Walmart Women's Accessories and the price was cut from $8.99 to $5.00. I had to bring it home, although I wasn't sure what I would do with it. One thing is certain—I wouldn't be caught dead with it in my possession, it's an old lady purse! I scrunched it up in my fist for the remainder of my walk so people driving past me couldn't tell what it was. It would look like I was carrying my heavy pleather sweatshirt. You know, the one with handles.

I always found something interesting on the dump road. I saw a lot of metal. Pieces of metal on the side of the road are Stratton's version of sea glass. Only these pieces aren't smooth or pretty or colorful or useful. If I were a metal sculptor, I would be rich, because I wouldn't have to buy material. Talent aside.

I ran this idea past my sister, and she thought I should go into the jewelry business.

Heavy Metal Jewelry was the name she suggested. Just imagine— Hubcap Headwear, Baubles by Buick, and Nissan Necklaces. The possibilities were endless! She said if she sees someone with part of a bumper on their wrist, she'll know I've made inroads in the industry.

I found a plastic Batman cape and gave it to my grandson for his Batman action figure collection. It was his favorite Christmas gift. Another time I brought him a toy car I'd found. The hood turned into a monster head and the trunk into the tail. The tail had been chewed, most likely by the previous owner, and my grandson noticed the mangled tail instantly and questioned me.

"Grandmother, did someone chew on this?"

"Oh, my goodness, no!" I lied. "It's twisted for whirling action."

He handed it back and walked away, but I wasn't insulted. He was never one for toy cars anyhow.

Well, at least the clothing on the dump road was useful. I found a wonderful hooded sweatshirt, and, except for the greasy tread mark across the chest, it was in perfect condition. And there was a cool knitted reggae-style cap that I wanted, but it was wet, and since I didn't relish the idea of carrying a dripping wet item home, I drove back to telephone pole number 743 to get it.

One summer day I saw a child's red wagon over the embankment. Two weeks later, I decided it would make a cool planter for the garden, but when I returned, the wagon was gone. So, I guess I am not the only person too persnickety to pick the dump, opting for the dump road instead. Maybe this is becoming a fashionable pastime. But I warn you, there are some tricks to dump-road rummaging.

First, I suggest some physical training—lunges for quick retrievals and squats for those "back up the bank with your loot" scrambles. You should start working out in March so you'll be ready for the spring thaw. Wise Treasurers (that's what we prefer to be called) know the bounty the snow hides, and we like to get out early for the first uncovering.

Second, you need a retrieval method. When you spy something you covet and there is oncoming traffic, stop and stare at the treetops as if you were bird-watching. Tap your chin with your pointer finger as if thinking, *Now, is that an owl or a chickadee?* Then, when the vehicle passes, dart after your treasure and climb back onto the shoulder before another car comes. If you slip and fall, just roll down the embankment out of sight and try again when the road is clear. If you slip and do a spread eagle just as a car crests the hill, lie still. Perhaps you can save face by pretending you were killed by a log truck. If you slip and fall in full view of traffic, hey, I can't help you. You're on your own.

Wait, a truck full of garbage just turned onto Route 16, and I think I saw something fall off the top—see ya!

Morning Coffee
with The Guys

This all started because Merrill's Market raised their coffee price a nickel per cup. Upon learning of this robbery, one of the fellas remarked, "I know where we can get coffee cheaper than this, and we can even sit down to drink it!"

So, the guys headed to the market across town—the one with booths and breakfast sandwiches. They meet there most mornings.

I was being sneaky when I joined them by not actually joining them but by sitting in as small a ball as physically possible in the far corner. I was staring at my iPhone, but little did they know my ears were at work, not my eyes, as I listened to their conversations. Eavesdropping was absolutely unethical on my part, I admit it. I hope, if you enjoy the things I heard and share with you here, that you can forgive me. Here are a few snippets of their conversations I was treated to in my sinful state of not minding my own business:

"So, Joe, whaddya think?"

Wise Old Joe admitted, "I get in trouble when I think."

Of course, being Mainers, they discuss the weather.

"It's going to rain until Wednesday, and then summer will be here all day Thursday."

These guys are retired, mostly.

"What are you doing today, Bob?"

"Nun-ya business!"

Bob's tone betrayed his annoyance with his immediate future, and his friend guessed what that meant.

"Ha!" he bleated. "You have to take your wife to Bangor, don't you?"

Bob's grimace gave away any hope of hiding the rest of the day's plan. The friend's bleating turned into shrieks of pure joy at Bob's misery. "And you have to take her to the Christmas Tree Shop!"

Another had a different job to do: "The wife wants the deck stained today, so I've got to get home and get the paintbrushes out so she can do that."

To which another answered, "My wife won't let me paint. She told me if I ever picked up another paintbrush, she'd kill me. She's been like that ever since that time she asked me to paint the windows. I didn't know she meant just the 'sills."

Then there was a discussion about owning a Plymouth Barracuda, initiated when one of those antique autos went past the large windows that front the store.

"I wouldn't want dust to get inside, so I wouldn't ever want to put the top down."

"I wouldn't be able to afford the tires."

"I wouldn't be able to behave myself in it."

The men discussed town happenings and our country's politics, but not to the point that their voices or blood pressures rose—the only spread here is in the dining booths, not the voting booths, for they are all on the same side. The opposing side, I learned, meets at the pizza joint downtown. The fellas also debated outboard motors, fishing spots, fiddlehead recipes, and how long to leave the fiddlehead stems when picking. It seems that is the way they keep the climate balanced and the friendships strong, and I wonder if that comes from intelligence or experience—or both. The meanest thing I've ever heard one say to another is "I can't understand how you're still on this side of the grass."

Then, when their coffee cups were empty, they left, but not for home—not yet. They had to go back to Merrill's to fill their gas tanks, because the gas there is two cents per gallon cheaper.

Psychotherapy
and the Waitress

I asked a college-bound relative about her major. She told me she wants to be a psychotherapist.

"You are a waitress," I told her. "You are already a psychotherapist."

She looked at me like I was psycho and asked me to explain.

I told her this story: People will come to you, not certain what they want. You will tell them they have choices. They will look over the entire menu. They will look at everyone else's meal, and then they will decide to have a pancake with real Maine maple syrup and a side of bacon because pancakes are thick and delicious and bacon is, well, bacon.

After their order has been placed, they will call you back to the table and tell you they need to change it. They think they ordered too soon and have decided they want a little extra something, but they aren't sure what. You will say, "Adding something to what you already ordered is fine" (depending on what that is) and you'll suggest they add something nutritious like fruit. "How about peaches or blueberries?"

"Of course!" Their eyes will light up with desire at the thought of getting something more, so they order their pancake topped with chocolate chips and whipped cream. They will be so excited, thinking chocolate makes everything perfect. They believe change is good and there is nothing wrong with a little extra. Before you give them this, you ask them if they are aware they are giving up pure Maine-made maple syrup for whipped cream. They look at you like you don't understand, so you give them what they request—a chocolate chip pancake with whipped cream and a side of crispy bacon. They eat it and are sated—for a while.

After they have eaten their bacon and half their pancake is gone, they will see the end is near and proclaim in a panic, "I'm not sure that's what I wanted!"

To which you will answer, "But that is exactly what you ordered."

"But, but . . ." they stutter, "I really wanted a different meal. I think perhaps I missed out on something!" They think long and hard about what that could possibly be and finally decide, "I missed out on some color! I have to have some color! I want a vegetable omelet."

They rationalize that because vegetables are pretty and nutritious, they are correct in that frame of mind, and besides, they tell themselves, "There's nothing wrong with a bit of change or trying something new." (Because it worked before?)

"Bring me a three-egg vegetable omelet," they insist. They abandon their chocolate chip pancake and consume the three-egg vegetable omelet, and declare from behind their napkin as they wipe their mouth, "Well, that was tasty, but . . ." They ponder, then realize, "It didn't stick to my ribs, and I'm still hungry." You suggest that maybe all those flashy colors aren't what they are cracked up to be and that they certainly don't compare to rib-sticking pancakes with whipped cream and chocolate chips.

They will be confused.

You will say, "Finish your pancake. It's delicious; it will fill you up; it's satisfying. You are even blessed with chocolate chips and a side of bacon. Millions of people wish they could have what you have. Stop your whining and finish the pancake you chose and be thankful. And besides, when you finish what you started, you will come to realize there's no room or desire for anything else."

They will realize you are right.

And that's what psychotherapists (and waitresses) do.

We the People

I was thinking. More specifically, I was sitting in my car in the Hannaford parking lot, eating soup and a corn muffin from the local soup cafe. As I ate, I was thinking about spending a whole bunch of money getting a few bags of groceries because one of my daughters recently accused me of eating like an old lady. I guess cheese and mixed nuts are nutritionally unacceptable if that's all one ever eats. Let me stop here and say I usually shop at the local small-town market because I am a firm believer that if we don't shop at our local shops, we won't have local shops. But I was in the city of Farmington, doing city things, so there you have it, that's where I was.

My plan was to eat my soup at the Prompto while the guys changed the oil in my Jeep, but it was the only vehicle in need, so all six men jumped on it and it was finished before my soup cooled down enough to taste. That's another reason I was where I was when I saw the folks I saw.

Eating soup in a car can be a messy endeavor. I had already used up three napkins from the cafe and was digging around the Jeep's interior looking for another one, soup in hand, which created a need for three more napkins, when I heard singing. I looked around and out my springtime, mud-splattered windows. A woman getting into the car beside mine was singing. Now, I've heard we are supposed to dance like nobody's watching, but are we supposed to sing like nobody's listening? Imagine a day doing errands or tedious necessaries and everyone around you is singing. Would that be lovely or torturous? I think it could go either way.

Another woman got out of a car opposite the singing woman's car. That woman was bogged down with essentials—purse, keys, cell phone, and glasses—and as she busily put those things away, that thing in there, that one in there, and that item in that place, the things took her attention away from the belt of her jacket. It dragged through the mud as she walked. I watched her until she was out of sight, thinking, "Man, she's going to be upset when she notices that mess."

Then a guy caught my eye. He was a rough-and-ready, motorcycle-type dude, gruff and tough and unkempt, with a scruffy, graying beard and messy hair that stuck up here and there like the hair on a koala's ears. Perhaps he purposely faced his day with a gruff-and-tough appearance in case a messy situation came about. Or maybe it was so people would leave him alone, allowing him to avoid all potentially messy human interaction while he was at Hannaford hunting for his food. I tried to guess which car he would get into. I guessed wrong and couldn't help but be disappointed in his less-than-gruff-and-tough off-the-bike-season choice of transportation. As I watched him drive away, I caught sight of a man in the car beside the motorcycle dude; that man was staring at me.

I took bites of my soup as I searched for napkins in the confined space that is the front seat, leaning this way and that as I rummaged through the glove box and the center console cubby, occasionally banging my elbows against the window or the steering wheel. At one point, as I stretched to reach into the pocket behind the front passenger seat, my rump took up the area intended for headspace. Each time I happened to glance the gawker's way, I noticed he was still watching me.

"How rude," I thought.

My soup was gone, and I meant to be, too, but as I gathered up my purse, keys, and cell phone, I realized I had left my reading glasses at home. I searched the Jeep for another pair I knew I had kept for just such a situation and finally found them behind my seat, under a bag of empty bottles intended for the redemption center.

One of the earpieces on the glasses was missing, so they lay lopsided on my face like someone or something had knocked me askew. I had prescription farsighted sunglasses to wear in the store and to decipher which aisle I was in. Then I used the broken readers when I needed to read little things like ingredients and big little things like prices. Switching my glasses back and forth, back and forth was tedious, yet necessary, sort of like shopping for healthy, non-old-lady food.

Aside from a watermelon tucked between the stacks of paper towels on the paper goods shelf, and a young man who had half a loaf of Texas toast on top of his head as a hairstyle, I didn't notice many interesting things inside the store. I spent big bucks on two bags of food—mostly blocks of assorted cheeses and cans of nuts—peanuts, cashews, walnuts, almonds, and hazelnuts. I decided, instead of buying one can of already mixed nuts, I'd combine the nuts at home. Perhaps that would convince my daughter I was still able to produce a home-prepared meal.

On my drive home I thought about all the folks I had noticed and wondered why I am so thoroughly entertained by watching my fellow humans. It eventually dawned on me, it's because we are messes. In this huge world, this vast universe of beauty and wonder and miracles, we, the people, are minuscule, marvelous, hilarious messes.

Seeing as how we are all one sort of mess or another, I was also thinking we should simply enjoy each other.

Ladybug Party

When the weather turns warm, the ladybugs turn out. I was cleaning one such day and had collected quite a few. I placed them in a group on the floor, with the intention of opening the window and setting them free, but before doing so I called to my young grandson, Aiden.

"Aiden, come see. It's a ladybug party!"

"Where, Grandmother, where?" his voice reached the top of the stairs before his legs even began the journey.

"There." I pointed a toe at the gathering of ladybugs on the floor.

"Cool," he breathed, and hunkered down to watch them. After a while it was his turn to call me.

"Grandmother," he said. He knew something I didn't. "This is not a ladybug party."

"What do you mean?" I turned and looked at the collection of bugs crawling around the floor in front of him. Aiden was gently nudging one of the bugs with the tip of his finger. That bug was upside down and lifeless, its tiny arms folded ladylike across its belly. "Nope, this isn't a party," he said. "It's a funeral."

The Society
of Cynical Sisters

There is a collection of kindred middle-aged souls who have spent their lives setting an example of how a proper woman should conduct herself. Having outlived the responsibilities of wife, homemaker, career woman, and cradle-rocker of the world, they are now in need of leaning a little left of propriety. They call themselves the Red Hat Society, and they celebrate fun, friendship, and the coming of age for women fifty and older. They base their name on Jenny Joseph's poem "Warning" that says, "When I am an old woman, I shall wear purple clothes with a red hat which doesn't go, and doesn't suit me."

The society, donning red hats and boas, travels in a boisterous entourage engaging in rebellious behavior such as telling jokes, playing kazoos, laughing, and having a well-deserved blast.

I have been pondering my choice of conduct for my latter years. My problem is this: I have been wearing purple clothes with red hats for decades. I have engaged in dissident behavior on a regular basis since middle school, and I often let go, laugh, misbehave, and whoop it up. I continually failed to set a good example for my children, and therefore relied heavily upon "do as I say, not as I do" as my child-rearing philosophy. I enjoy a lighthearted attitude, and

I am carefree, sweet, kind, giving, and happy. So, where shall I go from here? I think I must put on a different hat.

I will never again cut my hair. It will grow to my butt and I hope it will soon start graying. I'll wear it in a bun with messy wisps sticking out all over. Bobby pins and pencils will stick out here and there, too.

I'm going to eat anything and everything I want so I'll get plump and my elbows will have dimples that my grandchildren will laugh at when they poke their fingers into them. I'll attempt to slap their hands, mumbling something about disrespectful, unruly snots, but will never manage to hit my mark. The babies will be afraid of me.

I'm going to wear my trifocals on a pink plastic beaded chain around my neck, and crumbs from my lunch will land on the lens and stay there. I'll never notice. I'm going to be crabby, and my kids will call me only on Christmas and Mother's Day, purely out of duty, to stay in my last will and testament. I'll ask them half-heartedly, "What are your brats up to?" and, "What did you name that funny-looking one again? Did you have his ears fixed yet? One good wind and you'll have to drive to Matawamkeag to bring him back home!"

I'll lock my doors and keep my house dark on holidays.

I'm going to snarl and yell at the neighborhood kids as I threaten them with a flyswatter and will rightfully earn the name Crazy Old Bat. Everyone, even strong, young men, will cross to the opposite side of the street when walking past my house.

I'm going to drive a once-black, now faded to gray, beat-up, rusting Subaru station wagon with the back license plate askew because it's held on with chicken wire. I'll have two bumper stickers: "Winter Sucks" and "Screw Guilt." It won't even cross my mind that these are vulgar.

I'm going to cause road rage. I'll forget I have directional blinkers and peripheral vision. My top speed will be thirty-five miles per hour both in town and on Interstate 95.

From now on I'm going to wear ratty, baby blue slippers and patterned knee socks, all day, every day, even to the post office and grocery store. I'll be forced to shuffle to keep my slippers on. My outfit of choice will be a snagged and faded floral housecoat with a large coffee stain down the front.

I'm going to let my three chin hairs grow, and I'll absentmindedly twist them when I stand in line at the checkout. I'll use the ten-items-or-fewer lane when I have thirty items or more simply because I can't be bothered not to.

I'm going to talk to myself in public, and answer myself. Then, when folks stare, I'll bark, "What are you looking at?" or "Why don't you take a picture?"

The only issue I'll care about is me.

I'll start smoking thin cigars, letting them hang off my lower lip. I'll not be particular about hitting the ashtray, either. I'll spend my days writing articles for magazines such as *Old and Annoyed, Bygone and Bitter,* or *The Sour Senior,* earning only enough to buy food for myself and my seventeen cats, and seed for my three dozen bird feeders. I plan to buy a pellet gun to shoot the thieving squirrels, but I'll feed raccoons better than myself.

I'm never cooking a homemade meal again. I'll survive on Shaw's macaroni and cheese or pizza from a box. Of course, I can always share the cats' nine lives.

Does anyone care to join me? We'll call ourselves the Society of Cynical Sisters, and we'll wear whatever the dickens we please.

Just for Fun

The other day, a day full of business commitments, errands, chores, parents, children, and grandchildren, my friend Laura and I decided to veer off our course of responsibility to go for a hike and do some shopping. Not that we are rebellious (okay, I admit I am, but only in a good way), it's just there are those sunny spring days when the gentle breezes whisper our names and the boughs of the pines wave a beckoning call—a seductive song that silences our serious side, and we just can't handle being responsible for one moment longer. This was just such a day, and it turned into a day just for fun.

As we approached the trailhead we came across a guy in a field. He was lounging in a lawn chair in front of a helicopter.

Our necks slowly craned around to better view the odd sight as we drove past.

Laura stopped the car and looked at me.

I read her mind.

"We have to know, don't we?" I asked.

She nodded and backed up the vehicle. "Whose helicopter is that?" she called from her window.

"I was sitting here wondering the same thing," the guy said.

We laughed.

She defended us, "Well, we're going for a hike, and we wondered if maybe you were looking for a bad guy out loose in the woods and we should know where he is."

I was impressed with her quickness of mind to think of that excuse.

"Wow," I whispered.

"And if he's a good-looking bad guy, you want to know exactly where he is." Lawn-Chair Man's mind was as quick as Laura's. We laughed again.

We eventually found out it was his helicopter and he, like us, was taking a break; he from working on a mountaintop tower somewhere close by.

The helicopter was still in the field when we returned, although the Lawn-Chair Man was gone. Again, we stopped. I can't explain why, except that it's a helicopter in the middle of a field in the middle of nowhere and we needed to look at it some more. As we sat there looking, a car pulled up beside us. It was two young men who said they were lost.

"Do you know where Tumbledown Mountain is?" one asked Laura.

"Yes," Laura said, then fell silent, lost in thought.

She evidently took too much time to think, and the fellow impatiently asked, "Well, would you mind telling me where?"

Laura is one of the sweetest, most giving people I know, but she didn't appreciate being rushed as she tried to mentally map the best route for him, so she pointed across the valley at the mountain range to our east and answered, "It's over there."

We spent the rest of our day shopping in our favorite stores— farm supply shops, garden centers, and greenhouses. At the farm store, Laura tried to pet a goldfish at the koi display while I was tried not to gag at the collection of pet rodents for sale. One such pet rodent (a contradiction in terms if I ever heard one) had a sign on its cage that read: "This little guy will not bite you, but he will try to lick you with his very sharp teeth."

My burst of laughter caused Laura to abandon her fish and join me, where we giggled and laughed together.

It is now days later, and I am back to my B&B full of guests and work, but the memory of our fun that day, especially of the two of us standing at that pet display, laughing, still brings a smile to my face.

I am so thankful I have friends and days made just for fun.

Living the Life

I called him for help. I don't often ask for help, but in this case, I was lost without it. I called a computer tech support person, because I desperately needed him to help me untangle the web I had woven when setting up the website for my bed-and-breakfast. As it turned out, we didn't talk much about my internet problem; we talked about getting as far away from technology as possible. Our conversation veered off course when he started it with, "Did you have a good day?"

"Yes, I had a great day," I answered. "I ate well. I laughed. I skied."

When he learned I spend many days on the slopes, I learned he is a snowboarder. Our conversation naturally turned to that pastime. He lives in Tennessee, but his heart's desire is to live in western Maine. He's on the twenty-two-year plan of buying fifty acres on which to hunt, fish, and garden to feed himself and his family. He wants to live the independent, rural Maine lifestyle. His hope is to rusticate.

He'll be fifty-five years old when he gets out from behind the help desk. In twenty-two more years, he can live the life he dreams of living. He's working the first forty years of his life to enjoy the last, what? Twenty? Ten?

But what if you die when you're fifty-four and a half? I wanted to know, but didn't ask. Personally, I wouldn't trust time, but I didn't mention that either.

I know quite a few folks who are living the very rural life he dreams of—after all, it is historically the Maine way of life. These rugged Mainers live off their land, and they will work their acreage until the children take over or until they are six feet under. They farm from before dawn to after dark. They work through storms and scary times, through failures when the weather harms and through equally harmful government meddling. Is it worth it to feed others? The rest of us should make sure it is (for their good and ours!).

I have friends who are independent small-business owners—a precarious thing to attempt in these big-box times, but there is just something empowering and satisfying about being your own boss. One of those people in particular, although she loves her independent lifestyle, occasionally wonders if she erred by not taking a more worldly, secure route working for a corporation that has benefits now and a pension later. (I wondered aloud if that is truly a more secure route.) Hoping that working for yourself will work out for the best is a chance many Mainers gamble on and then work hard to achieve.

I knew an elderly man who shared his life ambition, his dream, with me from his nursing home bed. He told me, as a young man, he'd wanted to be the first in his family to attend college. He had hoped to be a doctor, but instead he spent forty-plus years as a milk deliveryman for Grant's Dairy.

I asked him if he regretted that path. He looked over at the portrait of his family on his bedside table with the conviction of a man who had recognized and fulfilled his calling.

"Not a single regret," he said, "not for a single moment. My life was meant to be providing for and nurturing my family, and I did that well. I was successful. Every one of my children went to college."

No regrets—the only way to live your life.

How to Tell

It has been written that the words you speak come from your heart. Often, these words are hints about who we truly are, how we are feeling, or what we are experiencing that particular day. Our world swirls around us, funnels into our souls, and drips out of our mouths in revealing words—whether we realize it or not. For example:

How to Tell When Your Daughter is Distracted

"Emily, what's the name of the song Holland was playing on her guitar Easter Sunday? I can't remember the musician's name, so I can't look it up on the internet."

Emily replied, "I don't know, Mom, but if you know the musician's name, you can look it up on the internet."

How to Realize Your Girlfriend is Exhausted

"This is such a big, huge world with so many things in it!" exclaimed girlfriend number one.

"Aren't you glad we don't have to clean it?" sighed girlfriend number two.

How to Tell Your Friend is Proud to Be a Humble Mainer

As we rode up the chairlift at Sugarloaf, a skier from away told us how he was looking for the perfect vacation home in our area.

His second home had to meet certain specifications—It had to be in the perfect location, it had to be built of specific materials, it had to have this, it had to have that, and so on.

My friend Cathy piped up and proudly announced, "We hauled our camp here from Cutler on the back of a dump truck."

The out-of-towner stuttered for a bit, and then asked "Do you mean it was a beach house?"

"Oh, no, no," Cathy explained. "It was an old clam shack."

HOW TO KNOW A FRIEND IS NIPPING HER INVOLVEMENT IN YOUR NEW HOBBY IN THE BUD

"Have you ever sewn a smelt to a fish line?" I asked.

"No, and your next question should be, 'Do you ever want to?'"

HOW TO BE REMINDED YOUR FRIEND IS A FISHERWOMAN

While at the University of Maine at Farmington's orchestra concert, my friend looked up from the concert program and asked me, "Which one is the bass?"

When I stopped snorting (because it would have been inappropriate to laugh out loud, I told her, "It's pronounced *base.*"

HOW TO LEARN SOMEONE NEEDS SUPPORT AND ENCOURAGEMENT

This past winter, while teaching a group of young people to ski, I watched one young man as he watched his fellow (and more capable) classmates ski down the hill in front of him. With something akin to hopelessness written across his face, he reassured himself with a whisper, "This is not a team sport."

If you listen with your heart to your friends and family, you'll hear a lot more than what they are just saying.

The Story of Harry

I said I wasn't going to do this. I said I would not write about my dog, but then again, I said I wouldn't have a dog. I said I didn't really want a dog of my own. I'm a cat person.

But here is the story of Harry.

I accompanied my pet-seeking best friend Laura to an animal shelter, simply to spend time with them. I had no intention of adopting a different best friend. Once there, I was invited to fill out an adoption form, and so I did because I didn't have anything else to do while I waited.

The form invited me to list the attributes of a dog I might be interested in adopting. I knew there was no dog in all creation that would meet all my requirements, so I gladly submitted the form with the following demands:

> A small dog only.
> Not a puppy, because I don't have time to train it.
> Not an old dog, because I don't want to fall in love and then lose it.
> It must be a hypoallergenic non-shedder (because I own a bed-and-breakfast).
> It must like babies and small children because my daughters have those.

It must like other dogs because my daughters have
   those, too.
I will accept the following breeds (yes, I actually stated
   this):
Coton de Tulear
Bichon Frise
Havanese
No yippy dogs.
NO POODLES. (Sorry, poodle people.)

I handed the paper in and smugly said, "Here."

To myself I snickered and said, "There! Good luck finding
that dog."

Two days later my phone rang.

"We found your dog," they said.

"You're kidding." I couldn't believe it.

"We found Harry in North Carolina, and Pilots for Paws flew
down and brought him back to Maine."

"You're kidding," I repeated.

"No, we're not kidding," they assured me. "Harry was a stray,
abandoned, and on the list to be euthanized."

"You're kidding! That's terrible!" I said.

"Come meet him," they said.

So I met Harry, a small, hypoallergenic non-shedder, kid-and-
pet-friendly, four-year-old Bichon Frise mix that didn't bark (much
less yip). Within the first minute of our introduction, he hopped
onto my lap and settled in, as if that was where he belonged. And
that is exactly how it felt—as if he belonged there.

I looked into his sad eyes and said, "Okay, I'll rescue you."

I didn't want a dog, but Harry was not doglike. He was more
like a cat, or one of those Hollywood dogs. He was fluffy. He fit in
my purse. My grandson, then two, knew the difference between dogs

and cats (because he has one of each), and he pointed at Harry and said, "Kitty?" If Harry was humiliated he didn't show it, probably because he is so pampered. His dog food and biscuits were softened with chicken broth. He got fed before I did. He went to the beautician and the manicurist more often than I did, too. But he earned his keep by keeping my feet warm—and by being the absolute best, most loyal buddy ever.

Yes, he was perfect for me, this cat-dog, even though that "mix" part I mentioned earlier—was most assuredly poodle.

You Just Never Know

You just never know who you are going to sit down with at breakfast.

One morning after breakfast, over a third cup of coffee, a guest and I were chatting. She mentioned her grandson, Aidin. I told her I also have a grandson named Aiden. We talked about how that name had, until recently, been rather rare. She told me her Aidin was named after his grandfather, who also had a rare name: Aidin Llewellyn.

I sat in stunned silence for so long, she must have started to wonder about my sanity. She tilted her head to catch my gaze and whispered, "Hello?" I shook my head to clear it and explained, "My Aiden's great-grandfather is also named Llewellyn and my name is Lew-Ellyn."

We had nothing else to say except, "Wow."

That evening some guests were relaxing in the living room, watching a movie called *Wilderness and Spirit: A Mountain Called Katahdin*. Another guest entered the living room and watched along for a few minutes before stating, "That's my movie."

"What do you mean?" the other guest asked.

"I filmed it. It's my movie," he answered. He was Richard Searls, a Maine filmmaker who has filmed several documentaries and full-length films.

Those guests were watching a movie that was filmed five years earlier while another guest, who happened to be the filmmaker, sat beside them.

And the next morning they all sat together at the breakfast table with Aidin Llewellyn's daughter and ate a meal prepared by Aiden's grandmother Lew-Ellyn.

You just never know.

Going Home

There is a saying, "You can't go home again."

This means, after you leave your country town for a sophisticated metropolis, you can't return to the narrow confines of your previous way of life. Because my new town, Stratton, is not quite a sophisticated metropolis and my childhood hometown, Greenville, is hardly narrow in its confines, being on the edge of a vast wilderness as it is, this saying obviously doesn't apply to me. I guess I can go home again, so I do, and often.

Going home is always an adventure, and this past trip was no exception.

My youngest daughter Holland, my niece, my mother, and a few other family members joined me for lunch at my sister's restaurant, Auntie M's in Greenville.

Knowing it was only a matter of time before someone betrayed me to Mama—telling her I had once again made fun of her in my weekly newspaper column—I figured this was the perfect opportunity to break the news to her first. I also knew I needed a few minutes of diversionary chaos as my only hope of escaping unscathed, so I dropped a bomb—I nonchalantly mentioned Holland was our maternal grandfather's favorite grandchild. (Family favoritism is a favorite, albeit volatile, topic in our family.) The expected ruckus erupted, allowing me to break the news to Mama. I did so quickly and with as much sensitivity as I could muster.

"I made fun of you in my Mother's Day column," I said, across the table and above the riot.

"Again?" she asked.

"I can't help myself, Mother; you're a nut," I explained.

"Bring me a knife; I want to kill myself," she moaned.

"Bring her a spoon," my niece said, leaving one uproar to instigate a new one.

Mama refused to be sidetracked. "You're making money off of me," she said.

I paid my lunch tab and answered, "Yes, I am, Mother. Suck it up."

Holland consoled her. "She writes about me, too, Mammy. You'll get used to it." (I think Holland is trying to become Mama's favorite.)

Later in the day, Holland and I walked to the family beach on Moosehead Lake, and as I watched her skip rocks across the glassy surface of the water, childhood memories of the days I did the same flooded back. It occurred to me that some things remain unchanged, no matter how much time has passed. The camp roads are still calming to walk along; the lilacs smell just as sweet, even decades later. The loons and the whistle of the train will always have that lovely lonesome call, and time spent with family is always precious.

In his novel *You Can't Go Home Again,* Thomas Wolfe intended to convey to the reader the unfair passage of time and inevitable changes to those things that seemed everlasting. Nothing brings that realization home more than seeing my old hometown friends looking now like their parents did when I was young. It's unfair that childhood vanishes so quickly and cruel that the place I am reminded of is here, where I spent it.

It's true—time passes, certainly and certainly unfairly, but the most important things in life never change, and you can go home again.

I recommend you do, and often.

SUMMER

Roots

We didn't know we weren't cool. We said the Pledge of Allegiance to the flag every morning. We ate dog biscuits on a dare. The summers of our childhood weren't about being cool. Feeding chipmunks out of our palms, eating blueberries that we picked from our own wild plants, and finding pink lady's slippers were the most important things to us.

My childhood summers were spent at "camp" on Moosehead Lake. No matter where my father's military duty took us, he sent Mama, his six kids, and the dog to Greenville, my parents' hometown, for the summer. "So we'd have roots," Papa said.

I remember arriving each summer. It was a trek from where we parked at the top of the hill down to the camp. As we made our way down the path, Papa's voice always caught up to us: "Pick up your feet!" He would yell this to warn us of the large roots that crisscrossed the well-worn trail. I would try to watch my step as I craned my neck around the box of provisions in my arms, but I would inevitably trip on one of the roots—body and box would fly, and the supplies would be scattered.

We spent our summers running around the woods barefoot, eventually learning how to do so without stumbling on the roots. By July, my soles would toughen up so I could soar through the forest not even wincing if I stepped on a pinecone, a twig, or a pebble. I would stop only long enough to brush the object away from where it had embedded itself in my skin.

The days were full of the business of being a child. We played among the tree roots, imagining them as our homes. I lived under a pine tree, and my sister lived under a birch. Our play was more creative than Mattel or Fisher-Price ever imagined. We raked and pruned, and the roots became our under-the-tree houses. We had freedom to roam, and Mama seldom checked on us. We had our boundaries and we respected them—the marshy area beside the beach, the fence along the neighbor's property. We were free to wander our wilderness, and we did so with zeal.

The lake was the only thing that seduced us away from the woods. We were allowed to swim when the thermometer on the front porch reached seventy degrees—it was the first thing we checked each morning. We burst through the screen door like racehorses out of the gate, and it slammed behind us. Mama yelled at the last child out—"Close the door ten times quietly!" The ultimate frustration was, in a rush to join siblings gathered around the porch post where the thermometer hung, you accidentally slammed the door on the tenth time and Mama thought you did it to be sassy.

"Ten more times!" she'd shout from the kitchen. (Mama was always in the kitchen.)

When the temperature and Mama allowed, we left the roots of the woods for the freedom of the water. I remember watching my sister hurrying to the lake, doing a bizarre dance as she stepped gingerly on woodland debris, her elbows fanned out like the wings of some strange bird as she attempted to lift her body over the rough ground.

Five of us children, seventeen grandchildren, and seven great-grandchildren live within a day's drive to camp. While we played among the roots of those trees, our feet grew deep roots of their own into the soil of Maine—roots deeper than those of Maine's tallest trees. These roots hold us here like they hold those trees in place.

119

They are like the arms of a loving father that nobody wants to leave. They keep us on this land we love and encircle even the generations that followed. My daughters are Maine women, and my grandsons are Maine boys.

My oldest grandson and I recently went to camp for a visit. As I watched him play around those same places where I spent my childhood summers, I could see the roots doing their job, encircling his feet and slowly growing upward to capture his heart.

The Pain in Painting

The paint on the farmhouse was old, chipped, peeling, or gone completely. When it was time for a fresh coat. I reserved a forty-eight-foot boom lift for the task. Painting season in Maine can be short, therefore lifts and other outdoor equipment are in high demand. I was given the lift for two weeks. It arrived on a Wednesday afternoon. The painter and his crew arrived early the next morning and began work. On Friday night, the painter went to a party, broke his parole, and landed back in jail.

One of his buddies called me.

"He'll be three months inside," he said.

After absorbing that shock, I called the lift company and asked if I could reschedule the ManLift for later in the season. "Ma'am, these are your two weeks. It's not available again until two years from now."

So, there were my options—none.

I was standing in front of my huge flaking farmhouse, ManLift in the driveway, unopened paint cans on the porch, a deposit of three-thousand dollars gone with the wind and I was completely pissed off.

Because it's often more productive to be pissed-off than depressed, I went into the barn, found some electrical tape and used it to write WO in front of the black letters MANLIFT, and climbed aboard.

(Making an o with electrical tape is tricky, but not nearly as tricky as learning how to operate a huge piece of machinery.) After testing several keys and buttons, the engine started. After testing a few more buttons and levers, and after being jerked this way, then that, I found the right one and began to rise into the heavens. Nobody really knows how tall and intimidating forty-eight feet is until they have been forty-eight feet above solid ground.

On my way up, I looked down to see my friend Jo, who had just arrived and was standing off to the side of the driveway, well out of the getting-crushed zone. She had a horrified look on her face, and was making the sign of the cross.

"I'm taking this to the back of the house," I called down to her. "Will you guide me so I don't hit the electrical wires?"

She nodded yes and made the cross sign again. She couldn't handle the stress and left as soon as I cleared those wires.

I decided to start on the top of the house while I had the lift and would paint the trim first because it was new wood that did not need scraping. I got into the lift, raised it and pulled the lever to go backward. In order to go backward, the lever needs to be pushed, not pulled—opposite of what you would think. The lift went forward with a thrust of conviction so hard, it hit the side of the house, and took a huge gouge out of the new trim. I stood there for a moment, stunned, and stared at the damage. I then lowered the lift, sat down in it, and cried.

"I can't do this," I said to my hands that covered my face. "I don't think this is a job I am capable of doing," I admitted to myself.

I have taken on big projects many times but recognized this one as beyond my ability. I looked at the enormous house and repeated to myself, "I can't paint his huge home! I simply cannot."

Just then, a small inner voice whispered, "You don't have to paint this entire house, but you can paint part of it, a little at a time, until you run out of time."

I went into the barn, got the palm sander, went back out to the lift, raised it to the damaged trim work, and with tears and determination, sanded it smooth. There would always be a scar there to remind me of this day, this story. Then, I painted the trim.

Two days later, my neighbor Yukie, his outerwear emitting a thick aroma of marijuana, stopped in. He's an old man, an old hippie, an old Maine Guide, an old taxidermist, an old everything, including what I was to learn, an old painter.

He put his hands on his lower back, leaned backward, looked up at me and hollered, "I lost about ten years to an alcoholic blackout, but I think, somewhere in that time, I was a painter. And I've been driving by your place, watching you paint this big old house all by yourself and I've decided, I'm going to get you some painters."

"Okay, sure, Yukie. Thank you." I said to him. To myself I said, "Whatever."

The next day, my house was like an ant hill—painters climbing all over it. Ladders here, there, back there and another over there. Two of the painters were young, voluptuous girls in tight shorts and two sizes too small halter tops. They climbed up and down the ladders, one hand on a rung, the other carrying a paint can and brush. Drivers passing at the intersection in front of the house gawked at them with eyes wide and mouths agape. There were several near misses of the ditch, and screeching brakes were heard at least once a day.

Yukie's group finished a day before the lift had to be returned. That inner voice spoke the truth—I didn't have to paint the entire house, only a piece of it. I looked at the freshly painted house. It was beautiful. I smiled. I was so happy, so thankful, so satisfied. I looked at the machine parked in the driveway, waiting to be picked up first thing in the morning. I climbed into the "WoManLift," raised it to the roof, and painted the front of the barn.

A Friend and an Apple Pie

It all started with a friend and an apple pie (and those two things should always go together). I had been operating my bed-and-breakfast for a few years when a friend of mine asked me to make him an apple pie. I had never in my life made a pie, but he was a good friend, a considerate man who was always available to help me out when a need arose. I would often arrive home and find my driveway plowed or a load of firewood deposited in front of the barn doors. He never said so, but I knew it was his doing. If he wanted a pie, the least I could do was try. I made him an apple pie. He loved it. He asked for a second apple pie. I made him the now-famous Caramel Apple Pie. He devoured it. He told another friend who came to me and asked for a Citrus Apple Pie—a pie his mother used to make him.

"Okay, sure." I answered.

I researched, found a recipe that sounded yummy and made my third pie. That friend told a woman friend of his, and she asked for three pies for an upcoming family gathering. She said she would trade me a huge chalkboard for the pies. Deal. Now I had a pie sign to place under my B&B sign—a sign that could be erased and changed daily with the type of pies depending on seasons and the available ingredients. I revised my B&B kitchen license to meet state laws and opened my bakery. I added a third "B" and became

Diamond Corner Bed, Breakfast & Bakery. Although I baked many other goods, it was truly all about the pies. I became known around town as the pie lady.

The bed-and-breakfast slowed down a bit during the summer season—gone were the snowmobilers who came to this area that

Showing off one of my pies.

boasted a thousand miles of trails and the second largest snowmobile club in the state. Also gone were the skiers at nearby Sugarloaf ski resort—the largest in the east. Summer brought Appalachian Trail hikers, paddlers of Flagstaff Lake, and random travelers. So, although the B&B had guests, it was a bit quieter and I was able to stay in my kitchen past breakfast, even all day on many occasions. I used to tell my friends, "I spend summers indoors and winter outdoors." (Mostly shoveling the porch, walkway, driveway, and roofs.)

People had their favorite pies—it always seemed to be the pie with the fruit that was in season. Rhubarb in the spring, cream pies for the hot days of summer and fall pies with the colors of fall in them—cinnamon, cloves, nutmeg and ginger. People asked me which was my favorite pie, to which I answered, "The one that sells." And they did—all of them. I had the dream that one day, one rainy afternoon, I would sit in front of the television with a Lemon Lush Custard pie all to myself, but that never happened.

After a few months of making the same pies over and over again, out of boredom, I started experimenting and developed my own recipes. For example, peach pie was popular during the summer months, and inevitably, I would have left over peaches come October. So, I adjusted the ingredients and made a peach cobbler pie. It is pretty and popular, like a high school cheerleader. Successful too were the combination pies—apple and peach, apple and blueberry, blueberry and peach, blackberry and blueberry, etc. Success was really all about two things—matching ingredients, especially spices, and using real food. I used the fruit from my gardens until they could not produce enough, fast enough. However, I used Maine fruit and real ingredients. I even made my own vanilla extract. The only canned item in my kitchen was evaporated milk.

The bakery slowed down in late fall—just in time to clean the B&B and get ready for the snow and winter guests. It surprised me that Thanksgiving was not a busy time for baking. I figured the reason for that is most people make their own pies as a family tradition.

One year running the bakery, I made eight hundred pies between Memorial Day and Columbus Day. And that was just the pies. I also made countless buckles, cobblers, crisps, jams, jellies, cookies. Oh, the molasses cookies! I would spend all day Sunday and all day Monday baking those yummy things.

Of course, like everything, pie has a history:

The original pie crust was not edible, A coffin, spelled "coffyn" in 12th-century English, referred to self-standing pastry made from flour, water, and sometimes fat. In other words, they were bland, solid, often rectangular dough-boxes. Like a sort of medieval casserole dish, coffins preserved the foods they contained and were rarely eaten; they were designed solely to hold the filling and there was actually more crust than filling. Often these pies were made using fowl and the legs were left to hang over the side of the dish and used as handles. The early pies were predominantly meat pies and a popular one, especially in the lumber camps of the Maine woods was robin pie—a pie that contained about eight robin breasts. We'll never know how they taste because it is now illegal to kill robins. They are protected by the Migratory Bird Treaty Act of 1918 and the Lacey Act of 1900. But from the mid to late 1800s robins were hunted, shot, and consumed. The Migratory Bird Act wasn't necessarily meant to save the robin from dinner plates, but other birds from fashion plates. There was an enormous demand for the large feathers of such birds as the snowy egret, ostridge, pheasant, and peacock to adorn women's hats. (Some milliners used whole bird carcasses on the headdresses.) The robin, and other small bird feathers, were not used as much, but this little sign of spring benefited from the law. And this is why I will never taste a robin, although I wonder what they taste like. Maybe it tastes like partridge or pheasant. I researched that, but not one article describes the meat other than to say, "It was tasty." I suppose trying to define the flavor of a robin is like trying to define the taste of a banana. It simply can't be described.

I'm certain there are a lot more foods that have gone the way of the robin—something consumed in the past that causes us to wonder, gag or shake our heads in disbelief. And it makes me wonder what foods we enjoy today that our great-great-grandchildren will be astonished to learn passed our lips.

Probably rhubarb.

Night Sounds Like Childhood

My bedroom window was open when I went to bed last night, and after listening to the chorus of peepers and crickets for a while, I was reminded of what it was like growing up in a house full of kids—noisy. I heard a dog bark in the distance. Yes, that would be Mama, barking at us to, "Keep it down to a dull roar!"

Our playroom was in the basement—a wonderfully spacious area with room and freedom to grow, and grow we did, through our well-fed imaginations. Those were the days of secret agents, and one of our favorite pastimes was bringing the TV show *The Man from U.N.C.L.E.* to life. My brother was lead secret agent Napoleon Solo, and my tomboy sister was his second in command Illya Kuryakin. My mind's eye can picture them running to, hiding behind, and shooting from the three-section couch they had rearranged and upended.

I was the girl they rescued. (I always had to be the girl that got rescued.) We spent a lot of time in the basement—sometimes too long. Once, when I didn't come up for a while, Mama asked my sister if she had seen me.

"Yes." she answered. "She's down in the basement, rolled up in a rug."

My brother had rolled me up inside a heavy, room-sized braided rug and left me there (to rot, I imagine). To this day, I can't stand tight places.

Lying in bed last night, I noticed the peepers fell into immediate silence when a car drove past. That was just like us, too. We would drop our toys and voices and run to the window, our noses just above the sill, to see who had driven in. I suppose because there were so many of us, we didn't go visiting much, so it was a big deal to get company.

A cow from my neighbor's farm mooed a long, low, deep vocal sound, and I thought of my father back in those days. I remember him sitting in the living room, one ankle across his knee, smoking his pipe and reading.

"Papa, how old are you?" I once asked him. I ran to my room and cried like a little girl at his answer, certain and terrified that I was to lose him any day to old age because he was so advanced in years. He was thirty-two. That seemed ancient to me, a mere girl of six.

I looked out the window, the stars above twinkled, and I thought, "Childhood is like a twinkle of a star: it shines as bright and is gone as fast. It's nice to remember those sweet and fleeting days, but I have adult things to do in the morning, a lot of mature, responsible grown-up work to do. I need to be rested. I need my sleep!"

"Enough of this," I told myself.

I got up and closed the window.

But I didn't lock it.

Smaller-Sized Servings

I sold baked goods out of my bed-and-breakfast kitchen. One day after returning home from errands, I found a note, written in chalk, on the glass window of my kitchen that read, "Pies, please!" I started setting them on a table on my porch if I had to leave for a bit.

I also began selling my pies at the local farmers' markets, and I found a small group of customers with a special need—smaller-sized servings. These customers were often older gentlemen, often widowed, and therefore, missing certain comforts. An entire pie would be a waste, because, unlike a young stud who might devour a whole pie in a day or two, these gentle souls had been brought up in the clean-plate-club era and taught that wastefulness was a sin. They were not willing to put their cravings ahead of their devoutness, but still, they craved and wished for pie.

Baking small pies would not be profitable and besides, I simply did not have time to create such labor-intensive products. I decided I could bake other smaller offerings. This is how single-serving buckles, cobblers, crisps, crumbles, and the like joined the pies on my table.

While researching these recipes, I learned there is a reason for the different names:

- A buckle is a single layer cake with berries in the middle of the batter—those berries give it a "buckled" (or indented) appearance.
- A cobbler has its fruit on the bottom with the batter on top. The topping may cover the entire dish or be dropped on by the spoonful, allowing the fruit to peek through and earning it the name "cobbler" for its resemblance to a cobblestone street.
- A crisp has a streusel topping, usually with oats, that make a crispy topping, hence the name.
- A crumble is a crisp without oats.

Pretty simple.

Pretty simple to please humble old men, too.

During my weekly trip to Farmington, I added a stop at Reny's Department Store to purchase one-serving foil pans and hopefully give the often world-weary elderly gentlemen a perfect-size pleasure. With coffee. On their porch in the cool of the evening. On a day that their bodies don't ache and their memories are sweet.

And then I learned about another group who needed smaller servings. I watched as a few young men, college friends, stood in a circle with wallets out, excitement so evident that it seemed like a wispy white cloud over their heads, as they pooled their money to buy a pie. I thought to myself, "These guys could also benefit from smaller servings, and I need to keep these single servings on the menu because these are the same men as the old guys—on the other side of time."

Mosquitoes

I have said and written before that guests were like snowflakes—
each unique. However, a handful of guests were much more like
mosquitoes just buzzing around my head on a hot, humid day in July.

Luckily, I actually don't have a lot of "mosquito stories" because
I did not let many through the screen. When a potential guest called,
I started the screening process. People usually gave themselves away
as troublesome guests by asking questions such as:

"Can I prepare my own meals?"

"May I have my breakfast at five a.m.?"

"Can I bring my ski-tuning equipment to my room and tune
my skis there?"

"Can my twelve buddies (who are staying at a camp up the
road that doesn't have running water) come to your b n' b to take a
shower?" (When I said no, the caller counter-offered: "Not even if
I don't take one?" My reply: "Not even if you never take one ever
again the rest of your natural life.")

"Can I use your ski-mobile?" (Me: "Ski-mobile? Um, no.")

And my favorite question of all time: "Will loud sex disturb
anyone?"

After swatting away those guests who gave themselves away by
phone, I did another screening when people stopped in to look at the
house, more specifically the rooms, as they planned for a future stay.

Folks like these:

After giving one woman the tour, she descended the staircase on her buttocks, slowly, one step at a time—like a kid would.

As part of the reservation process I asked guests if anyone in their party had dietary concerns. One woman answered, "I'm allergic to everything." (I meant are you diabetic?)

Still, despite my best efforts, a few mosquitoes made it into the house. For example, a family of four from Florida included sweet, happy little kids, but parents who were the opposite. "Maine's lakes are too cold," the mother whined. The father complained about the log trucks and that the fireworks started too late. The bugs (of course) were ghastly (especially the mosquitoes). He saw a moose but was disappointed its antlers weren't bigger. Every conversation we had, they grumbled. He wanted to know what Canada was like. I told him to go see. To my relief, they did, and a day early, too.

And the winner—a single, middle-aged car salesman from Massachusetts. He said the town was too "country quiet." He liked city lights, city action, and he wanted to know where the local bar was. He promised (with a wink and a snicker) not to "bring anyone back" to his room. He said tomorrow's breakfast time depended upon tonight's "action." He wouldn't pet the dog, but instead protected his fancy pants and nuts from her. He wanted to know if I was a "party girl," brushed imaginary crumbs off my shoulder, stood too close, and asked if he could "kiss the cook." He disappeared like a good intention on a sleepy Sunday afternoon when I mentioned the rifle under my bed.

Vacation in Vacationland

It's time for summer vacation—mine. I was planning earlier today and I had already called my friend Kim to ask what type of wine goes best with a campfire on the shores of Beech Hill Pond where she lives. I also called another friend to inquire about which shopping mall would receive all my money, then something happened—I took a break from my preparations and sat in my garden. As I sat there reading a new-to-me book that I paid fifty cents for at the Family Fun Days Craft Fair Woman's Reading Club Used Book Sale (in the "stuff" pile not the "fluff" pile), I realized I can't go anywhere.

The daisies and hawkweed that decorate the bank of Stratton Brook were in full bloom and the sweet fragrance of the wild rose bush mingled with the pungent perfume of the garlic chives and the heavenly scent of the tall phlox. If I leave, when I return, they will have left too. These wonderful aromas only grace me once a year, you know. The Blue Flag Iris has folded, but the Yellow Flag waves on and the patch of yarrow—magenta, golden, and perfect white—is not only on the edge of the border, it's on the brink of blossoming. Plus, there is a mystery out there in the garden keeping me here—a plant I think is a weed, but its fancy leaves are telling me it's not. I distinctly remember not planting it there, so I must stay and see who is right, me or it.

The tadpoles in the frog pond out back are going to trade their tails for legs any day. Who would want to miss that? And heaven forbid if I miss a truck on its way to the dump, just up the road from here, with a piece of wicked good yard art in the body. I couldn't forgive myself if I missed out on a great piece of junk because I was in a shopping mall in the city.

I don't believe there is a breeze anywhere that cools me as nicely or smells as home-sweet-home as the gentle wind in my own back yard. There is not a band anywhere that plays more beautiful music than the wind song of the silver maple leaves in the front yard.

I might miss a view of the ocean, but better to miss that than the view from my porch as my neighbors pass by with a smile and a wave.

It has been raining nearly nonstop for the past few weeks; I'm afraid I will miss the peace that comes when the rain ends and the woods stand in saturated stillness—borne from fear of more rain, as if the very leaves are afraid to move lest the skies view that as an invitation to open up again.

Besides, my email buddies will miss me.

It's decided; I'm going to cancel my travel plans and stay put. Home is where I rest the best anyway and that makes my land a very personal vacation land.

A Storyteller's Line

My storytelling days started in childhood when I told bedtime stories to my younger sister, Melanie. Those tales were fantastical and were about tiny fairy-like people.

Then, as a young adult, there were times my stories were less than honest. Although I enjoyed reading, I remember now with shame (and a bit of guilty pride) those times I skipped the reading requirement and made up my own high school book reports. Those were the days before Google, and because the teacher didn't have a web to search, I could easily weave a deceitful one. I received A's on those lies—a disgraceful bunch of A's. I'm ashamed that I am proud of those grades—proud because as a storyteller, I want to be told I'm a good one.

Somewhere along the line, I realized if it didn't really happen, I didn't really care, so I switched to and continue to stay true to my current genre—nonfiction. However, the stories I tell my grand-children are as vivid as their imaginations and include conversing with wild things and other improbable occurrences. (Enter creative nonfiction!)

One night, I put one of my grandchildren to bed (one of two five-year-olds at the time, as well as three three-year-olds. I tell you that simply because I knew it would be fun to write, but I digress.)

As I tucked this one particular child under his blankets, he asked, as always, "Will you tell me a story?"

So long as I have breath in my lungs and a beat in my heart, the answer to that question will be, "Yes, I will tell you a story." The story began the way they all begin:

"Once upon a time there was a little boy named . . ." I have learned to pause here so he can vocally insert his name, and then, of his own desire and description, he added, "Who was strong and brave."

"Yes, of course," I agreed. "He was strong and brave."

Then the story unfolds. My bedtime tales are usually about a young boy in Maine's woods or on her waters. They involve animals, danger, survival, and ultimately and always, victory. Victory because these men-to-be—without exception—will encounter failures in their lives, but never, ever will they fail within my words.

This particular bedtime was on Thanksgiving night, and when the tryptophan from the turkey started doing what it does best—fogging my brain—I told my grandson story number three was his to tell.

His story was of a boy, strong and brave, who went for a walk in the woods and came across a frightened, injured bird.

"Please don't eat me; I'm broken," the bird whimpered via the soft, innocent, not-worldly voice of this five-year-old. The little boy had no intention of eating the bird, but of course the bird didn't know that. The story ended with wisdom and compassionate dominion over nature. The hero of the story fixed the wing with tape and set the bird free. The end.

Except it wasn't.

It went deeper.

"Please don't eat me; I'm broken."

Those words had an effect on me. His words silenced me as I thought about the vulnerability of the broken, the defenselessness of the small. I thought about having the insight to recognize those who need help, especially those who, unlike the bird, do not vocalize their injury or weakness. I thought about having the compassion to rescue. I know people like that, people with empathy.

The poignancy of that sentence took me on a quiet ride that only literature can pilot. The sentiment stayed with me for many days.

There's no way this child knew the depth of his words. Those are the words of one much older, one who understands the human struggle. The only trial this child has had to face in his young life is a bossy little sister.

See, that's the thing about stories, about literature: One small line can speak to you, even if the author didn't intend it.

A Grandmother and Her Grandson

The relationship between a grandmother and her grandson is precious and should be treasured. Sometimes, however, the only thing you want to do with your treasure is give it away.

AND SHE SCORES!

Aiden was in a mood because I wouldn't buy him the set of pliers and wrenches he saw at the discount auto store. I paid the cashier for my purchase and called to Aiden who was sitting inside a huge truck tire, arms and countenance crossed. He joined me at the exit door.

"Aiden, please open the door for me," I said, aware that his mother is teaching him chivalry. Aiden opened the door just wide enough to allow his slender, snake-like nine-year-old body to slither through. It slammed in my face and left me on the wrong side and fuming. I opened the door only wide enough to allow my threat to reach his ears, "Grandmother is counting!"

Now, you must understand, when Grandmother counts, the universe stops—the solar system freezes in terror, vegetation dares not grow, and the entire animal kingdom holds its breath until Grandmother gets what Grandmother expects.

Aiden turned around and grudgingly trudged back toward the glass door.

I held up finger number one.

Aiden quickened his pace and, after reaching the door, reached for the handle.

I held up finger number two.

Aiden's eyes opened wide, panic plastered itself on his face and it drained of color. Sweat beaded on his forehead and trickled down his temples. He froze, certain his young life had reached its end. He was contrite, eternally sorry, begging me with pleading eyes to forgive and forget the number that follows two.

The cashier, who was watching us, explained his dilemma, "That door doesn't open from the outside."

Grandmother–1, Aiden–0

THE WRITER

Aiden is following in my footsteps; he wants to be a writer. Of course, when he asked if he could use my laptop to write his novel, I (being a supportive grandmother) said, "You crash it and I'll take it out of your hide!"

He spent a laborious hour hunting and pecking at the keyboard, his tongue working as hard as his mind and fingers. When he had finished and was in bed for the night, I couldn't help but take a sneak peek at his first attempt at story telling. In all that lengthy time at the keyboard, he had managed one sentence, *"Once I was spitting and then my Grandmother smacked me in the head."*

I GOT HIM AGAIN

I keep eye drops in my car. That means because of the cold climate here in Maine they are frozen most of the time, which was the case this particular day. After holding the bottle over the heat, I shook it and it made a little sloshing noise, so I knew the drops could once again drop.

"This is going to be cold," I said as I lifted the bottle to my eye. Out of the corner, I could see Aiden watching me, a worried look on his face. I dropped two in each and then stared straight ahead like a very bad, very blind actor in a science fiction movie.

"Aiden!" I said with panic flowing from my mouth and filling the car interior. "My eyes are frozen!"

Aiden's eyes were frozen too—stuck on me and wide with terror.

The gig was up quickly because I couldn't turn a blind eye to the look of horror on his face, and I burst out in laughter.

I'm starting to wonder why the child likes hanging out with me.

My Old Rocking Chair

Azra, her new husband Dragan, and her brother Irfan—stunning Bosnians with beautiful names—were guests at the bed-and-breakfast. Dragan was absolutely as hot as his name implies, and I could stare at him until fire shoots out of my nose.

"What a great name," I said when we were introduced. Azra, with an accent as luscious as the rest of her, agreed and told me that was the reason she had married Dragan—his name.

"Really?" I asked, disbelieving.

"Well," she said with a tilt of her dark head and a mischievous grin, "why else?"

Yes, Azra and Dragan did get noticed, but it was Irfan who had my attention. He was a photographer for *Dani*, a Bosnian news magazine that is the equivalent of, although not as famous as, our *New York Times* or *Newsweek*. After spending the past eleven years working in the Boston area, Irfan had returned to the country of his birth to be a part of its rebuilding.

One Sunday morning, Irfan was the first of his group to rise, the first one up for coffee (as movers and shakers typically are). He sat in my kitchen, in the old maple rocking chair that Aunt Rita salvaged from the Squaw Mountain Inn before it was destroyed by fire. The rocking chair she left in the house I bought from her when she moved to Texas. The same rocking chair I refinished one afternoon when my father took my daughter Kelly, then a toddler, to the family cabin on Moosehead Lake for a daylong visit. The rocking chair that held me as I held and rocked all three of my babies.

As he watched me prepare breakfast, he spoke about the state of his country. He and a generation of Bosnians were returning to a country in disarray, if not despair: a thirty-five percent unemployment rate, corruption, and all that jazz that accompanies a country shaken to its boots by warfare.

"There are many hard feelings between the factions," he explained. "A lot of people had family members die at the hands of people they now live beside. Generations will pass before the pain does the same, so it is hard."

We talked about the frontlines, and how country folk fare compared to city folk, and the difference in difficulties for the men versus the women or the children. He described the geography and beauty of Bosnia and talked about a dozen other things while I sliced pumpkin bread and set the table. I now know Bosnians do not have yard sales, they have piazzas, which are more like our flea markets. People, discouraged in their search for employment, search for family heirlooms lost in the looting that took place during the hostilities, then forfeit yet another meal as they pay to get those treasures back.

I asked him how the war ended. "Who won?" I wanted to know.

"Nobody won," he said.

"What do you mean? How can nobody win? Did they just stop shooting?" I asked.

"Yes, everybody just stopped shooting."

He shook his head as if he was just realizing that truth and all the realities one truth can hold.

We talked for a while more, until the oven timer buzzed and he joined the other guests who, one by one, descended the stairs in search of morning coffee. Then the guests, one by one, with a wave or a hug, left and he joined them.

All that remained that morning was me, my kitchen, and that old maple rocking chair.

I was always a bit disappointed in the stain color on that old chair. I thought it was too dark, and often thought I'd sell it in a yard sale.

Silly, silly me.

You People

I have been invited to Israel, Germany, Rome, Italy, and California. These invitations were from friends who, having felt a hearty welcome here at my home/B&B, found it in their hearts to reciprocate.

Isn't that nice? I would have gone, too, if I knew where I'd put my jeans. My second thought—after, *Wow, I could spend mud season in Southern California!*—was *I wonder where I put my pants? I haven't had them on in three days.* I haven't had to. I work at home.

Another bonus of working from home is that I never have to leave it. I not only have the good fortune of living in a turn-of-the-century house, but I am lucky enough to live in a housecoat.

Don't misunderstand. I work hard, I just don't look like I do. Working from home doesn't mean I live in luxury. It means I live in yoga pants and a T-shirt.

But there are exceptions. One day I had to exchange my slippers for boots and put on a jacket to walk across the street to Fotter's Market to buy a quart of milk and some carrots, then walk a quarter mile to Arnold Trail Service Station to get my car, which got new brakes. Next stop was the post office across the street from the garage, but I drove there, of course, because I just picked up my car. The new brakes allowed the post office to be my final stop.

The good news was not that my errands would be finished and I could return home and get back into comfy clothes. No, the good news is that I would be able to come back home, period. I never got out of my comfy clothes before I left. I daytripped in nightclothes. My preference for comfortable garments reminds me of something that happened last summer.

I was sitting at the counter at Stratton Plaza enjoying a slice of Hawaiian pizza when a gentleman from away started quizzing the owner, Carol, and me about life in a small town in the mountains of Maine. He was a businessman and thought this area was beautiful and, if he didn't make so much money in the city, he might consider living here.

"Like you people do," he said.

That was his first "you people." Carol is a proud born-and-brought-up-here local who doesn't put much stock in the opinions of folks "from away." Her eyebrows rose at his words. My lips wrapped around my teeth. He asked what "you people" do for a living here, where "you people" shop, where "you people" go to the doctor, the dentist, and the movies, and finally where "you people" take your dry-cleaning.

Carol and I looked at each other as if the notion of owning clothes that can't get wet was incredibly dumb.

"Do you have anything that needs dry-cleaning, Carol?" I asked, thinking there must be a flaw in my wardrobe, my lifestyle, because I did not.

Carol shook her head. I'm not sure if she was answering in the negative or couldn't believe I'd asked her such a thing.

I looked down at my Gifford's Ice Cream T-shirt and Walmart sweatpants and said to the visitor, "I think I used to have something difficult to care for, but now I just have a difficult time trying to remember to put on a bra before I leave the house."

Carol decided to speak again. "Yeah, that bra thing can be a real problem."

It was obvious from his pained look that the businessman was no longer sure what to think of "us people," nor was he certain he wanted to live among us, so he left.

I finished my slice of Hawaii in Stratton, in my sweatpants and T-shirt that hadn't been washed in two days, much less dry-cleaned, then walked all the way home—all the way back across the street.

The People of the Market

A farmers market is a wonderful place to meet people—and often, when I am at the market selling my pies, I meet people or encounter situations that are worth remembering. Most folks you meet are the usual hide-your-crazy types that walk to your tent, say a few nice words, purchase what they need and, after saying a polite goodbye, leave. Once in a while, an individual stops by and does or says something strange, or does something I would never have imagined happening, something that would make me smile wider than normal, shake my head, or wonder about the human race. The following are some of those times.

Occasionally, I would introduce an unusual pie, meaning a pie that most people had never heard of, so therefore were reluctant to purchase. When this happened, I offered free samples of the pie so those suspicious folks (who obviously hadn't learned to trust me) would know what delight their hard-earned dollar was buying. When I did this, the pie sold out before the samples were gone. Yes, the samples always outlasted the pies, except for one time when an elderly woman walked up to my table and, without as much as a smile or a "hello," helped herself to a sample of pie. She liked it. She helped herself to another sample. Then helped herself to *all* the samples, silently devouring one after another until they were all gone. And

149

then, without a goodbye, a thank you, or even a glance in my direction (I had been standing right in front of her) she just walked away.

I also met a woman who travels with her pets, which isn't unusual, although her pets are—a duck, a chicken, and a possum. The possum's name is Awesome because it's awesome. I don't know the names of the duck and the chicken; I didn't meet them; they stayed back at the house with the dog.

I met Awesome Possum and fed him pine nuts. I bet you think I'm nuts, but I have a bite on my finger to prove it—not proof that I'm nuts, but that I fed nuts to Awesome.

Too awesome.

You just never know what will sell on a particular day. At one of the markets, all but the chocolate raspberry cheesecakes sold. The weekend before, the blueberry custard pies were the last to go—then one day they were gone in the first hour.

One guy really wanted a chocolate raspberry cheesecake and kept frantically pointing at it, hoping, but his wife thought it was "too different." Her opinion ruled, so they bought a butterscotch rhubarb pie.

There was a woman who came to the market only occasionally and only for one reason—to bring me clothes. The first time she did this, she held a bag of clothes out to me and said, "These are for you."

I looked in the bag and upon seeing its contents, asked her what she meant. I am certain my confused expression would have asked the question without me speaking.

"They are your size," she said.

I thanked her for the gesture and assured her I didn't need them, that I had more than enough. I looked down to what I was wearing, to see if my choice of clothes prompted her choice of charity.

"Take them!" she sweetly instructed. I took them, never daring to question her actions again. She did this perhaps three or four times that season. I gave most of the clothing to a local church thrift store.

Some of the pies I made after I became known as "The Pie Lady."

Well, except for those two oh-so-soft-and-cozy L.L. Bean cotton house jackets, one of which I wear when I write.

At the market, the vendor tables were lined up in a row and folks strolled down the line marked for pedestrians by orange traffic cones. One woman did the same, only she "strolled" down the line in her car. She would drive through the pedestrian walkway, brake in front of the particular tent she chose to buy from, roll her window down and holler to the vendor to bring her whatever she desired that day. She would yell at me, "What do you have today?" I would walk to her car and recite the list, walk back to my tent, get what she had chosen, walk back to her car, and hand it to her through her window.

Many of the vendors and customers had safety concerns about her driving in the pedestrian lane and spoke to her about it, but that did not change her routine. We never found out why she would not leave her vehicle. Some wondered if she could walk, but others disputed that assumption by saying she had been seen walking into a nearby restaurant.

We have all fallen victim to that overly chatty, never-ending spewer of trivial conversation. We have all suffered from this situation we cannot escape because we are stuck where we are, in our vendor tents, so we have no choice but to stand there and smile and try to listen, although our teeth begin to crack from clenching, our ears start ringing, and our blood pressure rises so high that we are on the verge of levitating.

But thankfully we also have five nearby friends (in their tents) who, because they have experienced the same thing, rescue us by calling our cell phones to pull us away from that trap.

I was sincerely grateful that my B&B was popular and busy. However, because it was, and because it was located in my home, there were days when I needed some alone time. Time to answer emails, catch up with a friend, or just have a few moments to myself to breathe and think. On one such morning, I decided to grab that time by arriving very early at the Rangeley Farmers Market. I pulled into an empty field that would soon be full of vendors, tents, and customers. It was quiet. It was lovely. I sat alone in my vehicle, enjoying the peace and my coffee, when out of the corner of my eye, a man appeared out of the morning mist and stood at my window. A little unnerved, I cracked it open.

He whispered, "My wife sent me."

He hesitated, then continued, "She needs an apple pie."

I had to smile; he was clearly embarrassed. After seeing my reaction, he sighed with relief and explained his predicament. They were hosting a dinner party that night and his wife wasn't taking any chances that the pies would sell out, forcing her to make one. She had way too much to do to prepare for her guests, and taking the time to bake a pie would put her over the edge—and she was standing precariously close to that edge. She hadn't voiced a threat, but he knew it might be wiser not to return home at all than return without a pie.

I listed off the types of apple pies in my inventory. He bought a traditional old-fashioned apple pie and some molasses cookies, then left, a grateful, satisfied man. That made me happy.

These are a few of the stories I remember about the out-of-the-ordinary folks who came to the markets. Funny thing is, I don't remember anything worth mentioning about the "normal" people, except that they were, you know, nice.

Of Mice and Men

The woman slept in the guest room called Sea Whip because a woman traveling alone is sometimes nervous, understandably so, about staying in a motel. And since Laura was both traveling alone and nervous, she stayed in the B&B guest room decorated like a seaside cottage and therefore named for the whip-like, colorful coral, Sea Whip.

I immediately wondered about Laura. Not because she was traveling alone, not because her feminine cream-colored crop pants and pastel shirt were paired with worn and dirty men's work boots, not because she didn't have any luggage, not because she asked where the general store was so she could pick up a toothbrush, not even when she said, "I set out this morning for a drive and now find myself too far to make it home tonight" (home being somewhere in Vermont). I wanted to inquire, but I didn't intrude.

Her plan had been to come over this way and stay at her brother's camp, but she couldn't find the camp and was relying—unsuccessfully, it seemed—on a childhood memory of its whereabouts. I wanted to ask her why she hadn't arranged things with her brother before she set out on her quest, but I didn't.

She said she ran a farm with another person. I wanted to ask her with whom, but I didn't want to appear nosey.

154

She wrote on the guest registry that she was in the area for moose-watching, but Vermont has moose, doesn't it? I didn't ask her about that either.

Finally, the next morning as she was getting ready to depart, I asked her if she was going to continue looking for the camp. She admitted that she had, after eating supper in town, gone in search of and eventually found the cabin.

"You didn't want to sleep there?"

I was finished not asking.

She decided, with a deep sigh, to tell almost all. "I run the farm with my husband. Yesterday he did something to make me mad—no, furious—and I thought it wiser to pick up the car keys than to pick up a weapon, so I headed for Maine and my brother's camp. Believe me, if I hadn't found your b n' b, I would have stayed at the camp even though it is ramshackle and alive with mice."

"Eww," I said.

"Well, I would have," she insisted, "because I think sleeping with mice is preferable to sleeping with a man you want to force-feed rat poison."

We were interrupted by the comings and goings of the morning and other guests, and it wasn't until after she left that I realized my blunder. I had forgotten to ask her what crime her husband had committed.

Flying Tents

Attending an outdoor farmers market in Maine is full of adventure, from meeting new people to learning new things to realizing things you should have known.

What vendors use for weather protection is a canopy, but because most of us add walls, those canopies feel they have been promoted to tent status—and tents were invented for travel; it is their lineage. As strange as it might seem, our tents apparently know this because just a whisper from the wind can tempt them to take the wind up on an invitation to fly.

Canopies-turned-tents truly want to be airborne parachutes or balloons, and they try hard to make their dream a reality. They don't care about their earthly duty; they want to play on the wind. For this reason, we hold our tents down with weights. Most vendors used sandbags, but I used cinder blocks I found in the barn and attached them to the tent legs with bungee cords. Even so, out of the corner of my eye, I have seen a leg lift, threatening to dance away, and reached out just in the nick of time to grab it before it could escape.

This particular day was blustery. We vendors were not worried, tent-tethering experts that we were. We set up our spaces and started to sell while the wind swirled around us. But she will have her way, so on the tail of a particularly strong gale, she blew a whisper to the gust behind her, "Never mind the tents. Take the tables."

And take the tables she did. It happened so fast I could do nothing to stop it. I saw my table flip over on its side, and watched, helpless, as the boxes of pies slid to the pavement. Some boxes flipped over, completely ruining the contents, some pies spilled out onto the pavement, ruining just the tops, and some were saved by the sacrificed ones in the front, yet all were damaged.

I salvaged what I could, then sold the still edible, yet not-so-pretty, pies to customers or other vendors who, like one explained, planned on buying anyway but, since there was now a deep discount, decided today was the perfect day—piewise and weatherwise.

I let the birds have the rest. They swooped in and enjoyed my losses.

Then there was the day we were struck by lightning. There's not much to say about it; it was lightning fast. We all jumped when the transformer on the electric pole across the parking lot where we were set up blew up and started on fire. Then, the woman in the tent beside mine let out a yip and threw her umbrella in the air. The streak had evidently found the metal tip of her umbrella and sent a shock down the shaft to the handle in her hand. The fire on the pole died out, as did the electric service in the area. We shrugged, stayed, and sold our goods.

Because that's why we were there, to sell our stuff, come hell or high winds.

I'd Get Up and Dance

Live music from Maine musicians was a weekly summer event at the town gazebo in Greenville. The locals and summer folk who enjoy get-togethers and musical happenings unfolded their travel chairs or spread their blankets on the ground. They tucked lap throws around the legs of the old folks they brought with them and then made themselves comfortable as they waited for the show to begin.

Sometimes there was more than one show.

On one such evening, as I sat with the crowd, I watched one of the sideshows—a woman who danced. I could see her talent wasn't rhythm or creativity; her moves were an irregular, bouncy march in place, complete with arm pumping.

We Mainers are not so reserved that we stay home, but also not so demonstrative that we dance alone in front of a field of strangers, yet no one appeared to be pooh-poohing her. The only one who had the nerve to interrupt her was her little dog, and he did so loudly and with indignation. He yipped his objection at being tied to a sapling and ordered to remain still while she danced. She shook her finger in his direction and warned, "I am going to dance until the music stops. If you don't like it, tough! You just deal with it." She then turned back toward the band, pumped her arms, and bouncy-marched in place, a smile of contentment on her face.

I wondered if she was subconsciously speaking to the crowd that occasionally checked on her with a glance, because even though the dog didn't stop objecting, she stopped admonishing him. If so, the warning was unnecessary, because neither the crowd nor I were judging her; we were just observing.

She danced as though no one was watching.

Who would dance like that? I wondered. My memory answered almost immediately. There was another woman from another time, years ago, when I was a young nurse. I sat with this woman during the last days of her life. We had heart-to-heart talks about everything under the sun, but mostly about her days here on earth. She was free with her words, and I soaked up every drop of wisdom she imparted. One such bit of insight affected me deeply, so I wrote a poem about it and put it away for posterity—or for this time exactly.

"Old Woman"
Old woman by the window
day after day,
sees the same view,
not much to say.
She watches TV
and the aides in the hall,
she looks at the photos
hung on her wall.
She nicknames the staff
for mind stimulation
and fights with the doctors
over health indecisions.
She longs for her home
and not this state bed.
She begs for a pill
to quiet her head.

"Here you are,
at the end of your life."
(I can speak freely—friends we long have been.)
"What would you change
if you could live it again?"
She stops and she ponders
as she looks far away.
She remembers.
She thinks
of the choices she's made.
She tilts her head
as she questions herself,
"What would I change
if given the chance?"
She speaks with conviction:
"No matter who's watching,
I'd get up and dance."

Adjust Your Sails

My door was open, and through the screen I heard the wind fighting with the woods.

Inside, I was surrounded by people with opinions.

They sounded very much like the wind, fighting with the leaves.

I thought back to a time when my father and I were fighting the wind. We were sailing Moosehead Lake on his Hobie Cat. The gusts we were experiencing that day were caused by friction, as the wind's natural line was disturbed by the surrounding mountains.

"The art of it all," he said, "is learning to make the wind work for you."

As we did a quick come-about, he called back to me where I was "hiking out," tethered in place, leaning backward over the edge as a counterbalance, "When it comes to winds, you cannot control them; you can only adjust your sails."

Beautiful Feathers

Something got something out back; there are only feathers left.

Because I had watched a hawk swoop down and take a pigeon that carelessly preened itself riverside, I suspected it was another hungry hawk encounter. Judging by the pearl gray and white feathers scattered about, I think perhaps the hawk's supper was a Canada jay.

The feathers were lovely to look at, beautiful layers of subtle colors that change with the light and tickle the fingertips. They are fascinating to ponder upon; they are beautiful. Singularly useless, but collectively the catalyst for flight. I wonder if birds have an inkling of their magnificence. I silently thanked the jay for his departing gift. Had he not left them to me, my fingertips would never feel the softness of his wing, my eye would never closely admire the artistry of his being. I gathered several for display in my garden.

When it is time for me to meet my hawk, I hope I too leave beautiful feathers behind. Feathers that someone will find, admire, and wish to keep for their own.

In Defense of Ambition

I unfolded from my fetal position to lie like a starfish in the center of the bed in the predawn light. In semi-slumber, I pulled the covers snug under my chin and started planning . What will I accomplish today? What chore needs doing first? Then second, then third. How about fourth? My day was set out before I rose.

Like snuggling ever deeper into the comfort of the quilts, planning my to-do list brought a strange sort of comfort—a warm, fuzzy, proud-of-me peace. Having mentally planned my attack on the day and smelled the aroma of freshly brewed coffee, I was motivated to get up, get caffeine, and get going.

One morning before I began my to-do list, I called my youngest daughter, Holland, who was away at a horse show in Skowhegan. My phone call woke her.

"Hello?" She answered in a groggy voice.

"Hi, Honey."

"Mom?"

"Yes, good morning."

"Good morning. I have to pee."

"Are you having fun?"

"I guess so, considering I slept on a cot under a horse blanket in a livestock trailer."

She sneezed.

"What's your plan for today? Did you eat? Where are all your friends?"

"I dunno, Mom. I just woke up."

She yawned, and I could hear the morning stretch in her voice. "The day is a big cluster of unplanliness," she said. "I'll call you later; I really have to pee."

A big cluster of unplanliness. I thought about that.

Holland was awaking to a day of no plans. I imagined her wandering around, sipping coffee, with no destination or agenda. Just taking care of those chores as they appeared before her—grooming or feeding the horses—or doing activities as they presented themselves.

Doing whatever.

Come what may.

Going with the flow.

Following the wind.

Letting it be.

That's nice. Yellow happy faces and buttercups to her and all those like her, but that's not me. I like a day with edges. I like a day full of things that need doing. I like the feeling of accomplishing a job well done. I'm a go-getter, a doer, type A all the way, master of the to-do list.

I like turning stables into greenhouses, converting overgrown pucker brush into gardens, and making attics into third-story suites. I like making things nicer, more organized, more efficient. I like building stuff—homes, expectations, my business, and my future. I like work.

If my day didn't have a plan, I would feel as if I were walking around with my insides hanging out. Without a plan, all my good intentions would turn into long, slovenly naps. My desire to eat wisely would find itself lost in a plate of doughnuts covered in chocolate glaze. My goal to grow my vocabulary by one word a day would find me on the couch playing computer games for sixteen hours.

My predawn planning keeps me on track.

It's not as if my soups and CD collection are alphabetized, or I'm dusting the picture hangers while my family is strolling along the river. But *someone* has to plant all those dozens of flowers everyone else wants to stop and smell.

Ambition is good. It's fine to want the best, give your best, and expect to get the same in return. It's okay to know what you want, work hard for it, and expect to achieve it. It's not a sin to improve, to enhance, to finish, or to have a plan and see it to its end.

But I must stay balanced. I read a Bible verse that validated my ambitious quest for progress: "Whatsoever thy hand findeth to do, do it with thy might." But it also takes all my might (and God's sometimes not-so-gentle reminders) to prevent it from turning into "Whatsoever Thy hand findeth to do, do until Thou killeth Thyself and everyone around Thee."

So, I find relief in the realization that although it shows stable maturity to be able to stop mid project and go for a walk or listen to a child, to put your tools down for a moment to admire a bird in flight, it is also honorable to kick the cupboards because you didn't accomplish all you intended that day—then let it go because there's always tomorrow.

FALL

Let the Celebrations Begin

It is dark. It is as quiet as a sunset.

I sit, coffee in hand, waiting for her to rise. She's in no hurry, and I have no choice but to be patient, because it's not about me; it's all about her. She determines time and defines the day; it cannot start until she arrives. She is the sun.

As I wait for her to climb the backside of the Bigelow Mountain Range and properly show herself, I think, I wish I could rise as slowly as that lazy star. But alas, she lacks an urgent need for anything not of her own essence, including caffeine—a personal need that pulls me out from under the warmth of my bed covers. I light a lamp, pour a steaming cup, adjust the blanket around my chilly limbs, settle in my comfy chair, and open a book, an antique edition on bygone Maine folks: Percival Baxter, Dorothea Dix, Henry Wadsworth Longfellow.

I read. She slumbers.

I hear the haunting howl of a lone coyote just outside my window. His cry carries across the darkness like an evil spirit on the prowl. I look out, down over the hill, into the dark wilderness that is my predawn view. It is black. I hope his cry is not one of victory, although I know that is the way of life in this wild land. I have seen that necessary violence with my own eyes while wandering these vast Maine forests.

Maybe this beast feels lost in the darkness that is his kingdom and he cries. I imagine there are many kings who sit lonely upon their royal thrones. Perhaps some beasts—no matter how mighty—despair in their dark solitude.

The dog cries to go out.

"You will not go outside! Not until Ms. Sun glorifies the skies. Not until she introduces a new day and chases the wild back into the wild. You will wait. We will wait for her."

The sky above the valley is suddenly orange; she has stirred from her slumber and throws off the covers of darkness. Her first appearance separates the mountain summits from the sky.

"The dark clouds steal the moon," my grandson observed at just age four. This morning, as I remember his poetic statement, I whisper, "She does, too."

A moment later the clouds are no longer hidden by the black blanket of night; the pink she casts upon their underbellies hints her preference for this day-to-be.

"Is that your penchant for the day?" I ask her. She answers me not, for I am too far beneath her.

I pour a second cup of brew and turn my gaze to the east.

Suddenly, there she is.

Good morning.

We are free to begin the day.

Let the celebrations begin.

I open the door and let the dog out.

A Farmhouse Kitchen
in Fall

There is something comforting about the chaos in a fall farmhouse kitchen. Farmhouse kitchens are never truly clean or organized—they aren't meant to be. They are destined to be untidy, and mine was in an eternal state of homey busy-ness.

There are too many goings-on in a farmhouse kitchen for it to be too neat—cooking, canning, child rearing, and commotion—and these cheery spaces are made perfect by their imperfections. There are boxes full of things—mason jars, kindling wood, newspapers, or kittens—and baskets of things like cucumbers and zucchini waiting to be pickled. There is usually a bit of spilled flour here, a dusting of those lovely fall colors—cinnamon, ginger, and nutmeg—there, and a pot of perpetually brewing coffee. Because everything is being used for the harvest, nothing is where it's supposed to be. The rule is—unruly rules. On a counter holding down yesterday's mail is a cake ring, canning jar rings are mixed in with the silverware, and the ring around the sink refuses to disappear—it's like a three-ring circus from the rising of the bread to the setting of the supper table.

There is a rocking chair next to the woodstove for visiting friends, and something was always cooking—applesauce, spaghetti sauce, or spicy conversation. I learned to step over the cat, dust the

My kitchen where I did all of my cooking and baking..

crumbs out of the way, ignore the smoke alarm, throw my arms in the air, and let a fall farmhouse kitchen be what a fall farmhouse kitchen is happiest being—lived in and alive. And where there is life, there is mess.

I had a guest at the bed-and-breakfast who had been out on the road for several weeks for work. One of the things she missed most about being home was her kitchen. She spoke the truth when she said, "There is an anchoring of your soul when you are in your own kitchen." Although I can't put words to it, I understand exactly what she meant when she said, "I miss opening my own refrigerator."

I remember one November I was on a writing retreat at my friend Kim's Karen's summer place on Beech Hill Pond in Otis, a small town just north of Ellsworth. While there, I prepared Thanksgiving dinner for my family in her kitchen. As lovely and outfitted as her kitchen was, I decided that cooking in another woman's kitchen is like kissing another woman's man. And anything cooked up outside your own kitchen just doesn't taste as good.

My fall garden was an extension of the kitchen chaos, and I lost control. Before I could put my hand to the highbush cranberries meant for my jelly, those greedy birds were stealing them all. The squash not yet harvested was threatening to become squish. The rose hips were begging to come in for tea, the potatoes must have thought I'd left for The County, and at any moment, four thousand more tomatoes were going to ripen. I thought the harvest dance was going well, but a morning's stroll through the garden showed me that I had missed a few beets.

I learned to throw my hands in the air and let my garden be what it was meant to be—a barely tamed child. Just like my fall kitchen.

An Extra Chair

Farmers markets in small-town Maine are often a social affair. Not only did my friends stop by for a visit and to replenish their pantries, but regular customers eventually became close friends. For this reason, I always set an extra chair in my booth. It was for friends or, in one instance, for the daughter of a friend. My friend would leave her little girl with me while she shopped, and the child would content herself, sitting in the chair playing with her stuffed kitten "Fluffy Fluff." Fluffy Fluff had large plastic pink eyes, a pink purse with a matching pink sweater, and a beaded bracelet. This stuffed animal had all any child with an imagination would need to be entertained long enough for Mom to finish her market to-do list.

Somedays, if everyone was busy, the extra chair stayed empty. Other days, it was the chair that was busy, as one, then two, then three friends stopped by for a visit. Typically, if I had a chance to sit, it wasn't for long as I would again be standing, tending to customers and occasionally, during those times, I would turn around to see both my chair and the extra chair occupied by chatting friends.

It was the habit of all the vendors to ask their neighbor to watch over their tent while they did the "walk-around"—a saunter around the market for a short visit with the other vendors, to say hello and to see what was new on their table or in their life. It could easily be a new tractor, a new variety of vegetable, a new cow, or a new grandchild.

The markets became fun social times and I continue to be friends with many, many people who I met there. These are friends I still meet for lunch. We laugh together, share with each other, learn from each other, and love each other. The friendships will last a lifetime all because someone needed tomatoes and there was an extra chair.

A Day of Wonder

The roof was standing-seam steel, I was told. Lasts a hundred years is what else I was told. All I know is it needed a paint job and the folks I bought the house from must have thought so too, because there were several cans of unopened roof paint in the cellar. I wondered why that job had never been done.

I found a painter who would tackle the roof for me, using the paint in the cellar. I would lug it out from the cellar for him.

One thing that got in the way of me lugging the cans from the cellar was the appearance of three south-bound backpackers on my doorstep, all looking for a ride to Rangeley. They were hiking the Appalachian Trail. One of them had an injury of some sort, so the three, obviously being musketeers, stuck together and took a zero-miles day to visit a doctor.

This group included a physics specialist, a civil engineer, and a scientist (the one who was hurt). The physics guy was from Liverpool, England, and no, he never met any of the Beatles. I think half of the Beatles were dead by the time he was born anyway.

"Why in the world are three brains wandering around in the Maine wilderness?" I asked. I'll tell you what I learned—they are new brains, fresh-out-of-college professional brilliance that can't find a job. Well, not the scientist, the hurt one; he was just a junior, a scientist-to-be, yet he was so smart it made my face scrunch up when he spoke.

They said they heard I shuttle hikers, which isn't true. But that untruth probably got around town as gospel because someone saw me dropping off a hiker at the trailhead the previous Sunday morning. I wondered who witnessed that.

I told the three musketeers that I was waiting for my roof painter to show up. They said they would pay me forty bucks and the cost of gas. I said, in that case, my painter could wait for me and we all went to Rangeley.

When we got to Rangeley, the scientist went to the doctor. While we waited, I went to the bookstore with the two others. Because they were from Maryland, the local libraries wouldn't lend them books.

While we were at the bookstore, I met an old friend I hadn't seen in at least five years. I received the best hug of the month right by the book of the month. At the bookstore, I met a couple of new folks who, in five years or so, will be old friends, too—no doubt in my mind. The hikers and I went to lunch and enjoyed an interesting meal and delicious conversation.

They mentioned that they noticed immediately upon entering our little town that there were employment opportunities up for grabs—construction flaggers—for a whopping nine bucks per hour. "Yup, and no takers," I told them.

They wanted to know why.

"Could be the road dust, could be the requirement of standing all day, could be the competing social programs," I told them. The physics guy said something, but it was in English and I couldn't understand his accent. I think he said he was once a techie for the opera.

The three were thinking of becoming flaggers. Just kidding. They were trying to decide whether or not to continue the Appalachian Trail south from Rangeley, skipping the Stratton to Rangeley part, or to stick to their puritan ways and back track, then make tracks back. The only thing they knew at that moment was that they were ready to get back to hiking, even though the injured scientist had not been able to see the doctor because he didn't have an appointment. I wondered if his injury was bad enough to end his hike.

We all drove back to Stratton, to the AT trailhead just south of town. As I neared the B&B, I could see the painter at work on the roof. I wondered what his thoughts were when he entered my home and retrieved the paint from the basement.

You never know what a day will bring, but guaranteed, it's always a wonder.

Gardens Are Important

There was a family of three staying in my yard, in their camper. They didn't want to stay in the B&B because they wanted to bring their dogs, and Holland's dog, Sadie, would not be happy sharing attention with another pup. So they used our electrical outlet and, for a small fee, stayed in the yard. It sort of looked like a campground with the camper out there along Stratton Brook. The father and son went hiking in the Bigelow Mountains. The mom lazed in bed, read, and listened to the babbling brook.

My gardens were a big part of the bed-and-breakfast. There were Adirondack chairs and benches along the brook, which meanders past the house on its way to Flagstaff Lake. Guests often sat and enjoyed the waterfront, the scenery, and the wildlife, especially the beaver family that lived nearby. The adult beavers, who mate for life, came upstream every evening around six o'clock. I suppose they had been in the lake all day, fishing. When the parents got home, the young beavers came out of hiding and ate the apples that had fallen from the tree. They rolled them down the bank into the water, then slid down themselves and enjoyed their snack while floating around. It was a delightful scene, especially for city folks.

Many guests enjoyed their morning coffee in the yard and several brought lunch back from the local deli, spread out a blanket, and picnicked there. They loved the birds that visit the feeders and the flowers (that daily graced their rooms and the breakfast table). It wasn't unheard of to have non-guests walk along the river's edge or rest in the shade of the huge elm tree.

I purchased two fourteen-foot canoes and two sit-on-top kayaks, as well as paddles and life jackets for guests to use. They could put in at Stratton Brook from the small dock in the garden for an easy, relaxing paddle to Flagstaff Lake. Many summer evenings, after baking in a hot kitchen all day, I would escape to the cool water in a kayak, paddle upstream to the dam, then lay back, allow myself to drift down the brook and drift off to a snooze until I hit something—usually the bridge. I woke up cooled down and refreshed.

Another big part of my bed-and-breakfast business was the vegetable garden. I admit to being a novice gardener, but found raising vegetables a rewarding and satisfying activity. I got hooked on growing and learned from friends, neighbors, and especially the farmers at the farmers market I attended with my baked goods.

Of course, the local ladies were full of valuable information. When I first moved in, I was flummoxed by the huge bin full of sand in my cellar. I told one of the elderly farm ladies about the family-sized litter box. She very sweetly explained that it was a box for winter vegetable storage. Another woman in town asked me why I didn't harvest the highbush cranberries from the bush in the yard. My answer was easy—I had no inkling that they were edible. She told me not to harvest them until after the first hard frost. From that day on it was a contest between me and the bohemian waxwings and cedar waxwings as to who would get the berries when they were ready. I lost more often than I won.

I used ingredients from the gardens in my baking, and guests enjoyed knowing that, and also that everything was fresh and made from scratch. I grew rhubarb for my "Meet Your Sweetie by the Rhubarb Patch" bread, raspberries for my "Out Back" raspberry jam, zucchini for my chocolate chip zucchini bread, highbush cranberries for my "Can't Reach the High Bush" cranberry jelly, squash for winter squash bread, and delicious squash soup for my winter suppers.

One guest who was city born-and-raised noticed a package of meat on the counter with a label that read "moose burger" and some just-harvested dirty vegetables laying in my sink. He had a question. "Maine folks really eat this way?"

I answered, "Ayuh."

Deer grazed in the backyard, much to the guests' delight, but I had to protect the veggie garden from them with eight-foot-high netting. That kept the deer out, but did not deter the groundhogs. One summer in particular they were so destructive, they were threatening not only my livelihood, but my winter food cache! Sneaky little buggers that they were, I could not catch them in the act. Then one morning, I was in my bedroom and happened to glance out the window that overlooked the backyard and garden. A groundhog was weaseling under the fence, heading for his breakfast. I knew by the time I got out there, he would be gone, so I grabbed my rifle from under my bed, opened the window, aimed, fired, and got him.

Then I remembered it is illegal to fire a weapon within town limits. Oops.

Someone must have heard the shot and called the cops because a cruiser showed up and parked at the historical society building across the street, their window down, no doubt waiting for a second shot to be fired so they would know where or who or what.

I wasn't about to confess, so I went out, cranked up the riding mower and innocently mowed the lawn.

To the Holy Land

Traveling in Maine is easy if you take the interstate. I hate the interstate. It doesn't have any character. It's boring. It's bland land. Yes, it gets you where you are going as quickly as possible, but I also dislike rushing things—like maniacs from away in fast cars and eighteen-wheelers passing me at high rates of speed. I like going slow and looking at the Maine countryside. I enjoy taking my time, going to those places that have stop signs but no vehicles to stop for. I like sauntering.

I had recently learned a story about the word saunter. Someone said it came from pilgrimages to the Holy Land in the Middle Ages. People who passed through tiny villages along their journey were asked where they were going. "À la sainte terre," they would answer. "To the Holy Land." They became known as sainte-terre-ers or saunterers. Saunter has also been connected with the Middle English word aunter, or adventure, and may also represent the French aventurer, "to venture." Whichever it is, I think all are beautiful—almost as beautiful as Maine's byways, and while sauntering around the state, I find the most interesting people and places.

Because I love our Maine countryside, I was looking for a scenic route between the two places I had to be that particular day—Oakland and Bangor. This, and the mysterious disappearance of my *Gazetteer*, is what prompted me to stop and ask locals for their opinions on any nearby scenic routes. My hunger is what motivated me to stop at Two Guys in a Trailer Grill, which sounds exactly what it is—a trailer turned into a takeout eatery with two guys cooking and serving the meals. I thought the name of the grill was oddly perfect in its Maine-ness.

The two guys made my lunch, but couldn't answer my question. They directed me to the guy in the tent "over there," on the other side of the parking lot. "He might know," they said.

I sat at the stark picnic table that sat on the parking lot pavement in front of the trailer grill and ate my meal, then walked to the tent where a bearded man was selling antiques and whatnots. I asked him if he could suggest a scenic route between Oakland and Bangor.

"The map software on my iPhone refuses to suggest anything but the interstate," I explained.

"I don't know; I'm a lobsterman," was his gruff answer.

That made complete sense to me, although why a lobsterman was selling antiques and whatnots out of a tent near Oakland did not. I stifled my questions and figured he was simply cleaning out his late mother's house. Or selling old stuff is his side job or perhaps his boat sank. I'll never know.

I was on my own, so I set out and headed somewhat north and east and then north again and sort of eastward, knowing I would, as always, end up where I am supposed to be, albeit probably not on the day I'm supposed to be there.

What I saw on my journey was poetry in its simplicity. I viewed Grange Halls, apple orchards, and pumpkin patches. Majestic sunflowers lining the edge of tired gardens, bowing their heads to the sun as they gave up their seeds and their season. Red barns, rebel flags, and overgrown rhubarb patches. The crumbling, moss-covered headstones of bygone generations, abandoned and rusting tractors in fields with no end. Winter firewood neatly stacked near the kitchen door on wraparound porches. Rock fences, country churches with stately steeples, hills and valleys and small-town markets with anti-quated gas pumps standing stubbornly against the ravages of time. A handmade, hand-painted HONEY FOR SALE sign at the end of a gravel driveway that led to an old farmhouse, the warm glow of a lit lamp in the window warding off the darkness of dusk and loneliness. A harvest moon rising behind the home, taking its place to silence the day and rule the night.

What I saw on this back road saunter through Maine is art that I imagine every artist hopes to create. I saw a mural of rural Maine, the Holy Land.

Falling Behind the Garden

The garden's bounty kept me so busy in the fall that I didn't have time to feed my family. The garden, like life here in the mountains of Maine, went wild. The kitchen was jam-packed with so many blackberries and blueberries, zucchini, squash, cabbages, cucumbers, tomatoes, and beets that there was no room to sit down to eat any of it. I spent all my time chopping, shredding, canning, preserving, freezing, and complaining to the family that they need to get out of my way by getting out of my kitchen.

Not everything that grew out there made it to the kitchen. There was this greenish-yellowish-pinkish round thing growing out of an unmarked garden plot—and that made me think of an "unmarked grave," which made me nervous. I left it alone. It did the same for me.

I spent every spare moment filling the freezer and root cellar with food to fill us this winter. My answering machine message said, "I'm in the garden. Leave your name and number and I'll call you in December."

I wondered if a conveyer belt from the garden gate to the kitchen window would be a worthwhile project.

One night, I had a dream. A cornucopia of vegetables challenged me to come up with yet more recipes for them. In my dream they grew mouths and chanted,

"You don't know what to do with us."

"You don't know what to do with us."

"You don't know what to do with us."

The first thing I did the next morning was to ask Google, "What can I do with fifty thousand cherry tomatoes?"

Google answered, "Ask Jeeves."

Jeeves suggested I spike them with vodka. Jeeves handles a problem the same way many people do—with alcohol.

Being in such a vegetative state made me unable to prepare a meal. One day, Holland and three of her friends spent the entire afternoon moping around the kitchen, sidestepping baskets of acorn squash and bushels of butternuts, getting under my feet, and brooding over my head to each other:

"What can we eat?"

"I don't know. What do you want to eat?"

"I don't know. What is there to eat?"

"I don't know. Nothing."

What they did know is when I'd had enough of them acting like fruit flies in my kitchen and they needed to skedaddle. They wisely took my advice and my money and went to the Stratton Diner across the street.

Two hard frosts later, the season was finished. The tomatoes were canned, and the squash was soup. I stared out the window at the lifeless garden. The only thing that remained were the vines that, just a few weeks ago, pumped life into the pumpkins. Now they look like large strands of cooked spaghetti—the garden was done. I started thinking about next year. *I bet I could grow some corn and beans, perhaps some okra and peppers. Of course, I'd have to make the garden a little bit bigger.*

Fear of Trying

Howard, a friend and fellow gardener who lives in Virginia, enjoys a growing season that lasts several months longer than mine, but evidently it's still not long enough to grow butternut squash. He told me he doesn't grow that particular vegetable because it takes about one hundred days for it to reach maturity. I didn't know that. He told me this after I had already planted mine in the ground—roughly eighty days before my zone's killing frost. The crop would fail before it even had a chance to succeed.

It seems to me there is more reason to fear success than failure. If you fail, you can give up and move on to something else. If you succeed, you have more work to do. For example, if you succeed at growing butternut squash, you now have a crop to harvest, cook, store, or preserve. Then you have next year's crop to plan for because now you have a reputation for growing great squash and maybe have been voted Butternut Squash Queen of the county. If, however, you fail on your first attempt, the only effort that remains is shrugging your shoulders and sighing, "Oh, well, perhaps I'll plant kohlrabi."

When my oldest daughter, Kelly, was in middle school, she medaled in track at every meet. You can imagine my shock when she came to me and asked permission to quit the team.

"Why on earth do you want to quit?" I asked her. "You place every time!"

"Exactly, that's why I want to quit. It's too much stress; once you have medaled, you can never *not* medal!" she complained. Well, she was wrong, but she had a point—success has its downfalls.

There's not much that frightens me these days, but I didn't always have my current "jump in without looking to see who is watching" attitude. There was a time when I actually feared trying. When I was younger, I refused to learn to dive.

I was staying at a Holiday Inn with my family, when my father asked from beside the pool, "Why don't you dive?"

"I prefer to jump, Papa. If I dive, I might bang my head," was my excuse.

My father could see straight through to the faintheartedness of the matter and called me to his side.

"You aren't afraid of diving," he said. "What you are is afraid of what people will think of your attempt. I'm going to tell you the secret to overcoming the fear of looking foolish—you are never, for the rest of your life," he gestured to the strangers around the pool, "going to see these people again. Now, get out there, put your head down, your hands in front of you, and dive in."

Ever since that day, I dive into things on a regular basis, always with my head down and my hands clasped in front of me, always with the thought that I'm never, ever, for the rest of my life, going to see those people again.

Success and failure aren't always what we imagine. Success isn't necessarily the end of a thing and failure is not a disgrace. But fear of trying is.

Blooming Out of Season

Yesterday was a rare warm day in late November. I went for a walk along a leaf-covered country road with Sadie. This is the season when Sadie is the same rust color as the frost-bitten ferns, fallen leaves, and pine needles. As she walked beside me on the shoulder of the road, she blended so well with our surroundings that at times I had to look twice to make certain she was still there.

This autumn earth whispers to me of the winter that will soon arrive. There are flocks of migrating geese and old geezers on their way to warmer climes. The flap of a blue tarp covering a readied firewood pile is reminded by a gentle breeze to wave goodbye to fall and it makes a forlorn rustling noise as it does. Everything but today's mild temperature speaks of the cold to come. The sun is warm on my back as I walk. Soon the only warmth I will feel in the outdoors will be from the heat of my snowmobile's engine.

I lift my head to fully breathe in the bittersweet smell of a woodsy world preparing to go into an icy sleep. I am not mourning for the season past because this season and the one ahead are for a time of rest—or so I thought until I saw her. I knew she was a lady; she was dressed in pink. A lone Lady lupine adorned in bicolor petals, planted firmly in her belief that not June, but late November is her time to shine. Even the purple asters and yellow sunflowers know enough to fade away, but not her, not yet. She blooms brilliantly even though she blooms alone. There she stands in all her glory, out of her season.

I wonder where she was when the hillside surrounding her was alive with lupines. Was she being lazy and sleeping in? Was she being naughty and playing hide-and-no-seed? Was she in bondage in a place she could not grow? Was she lost? Was she struggling in the weeds? The reason does not matter, because she is here now, more beautiful than she would have been had she appeared with a hundred others just like her. She is so beautiful in fact that her loveliness silences all my questions. The world and I do not need to know why she is a late bloomer, for she is finally standing tall, on her own in the sun, more of a blessing as one, than as one in an army of thousands.

The Root Cellar

I baked the last butternut squash for my Italian-sausage-and-squash soup.

It's a melancholy feeling to consume the last thing from the garden—it's like saying goodbye to a friendship that has run its course. I was thinking, as I skinned this, my last squash, and there was a touch of sadness in my voice when I spoke to Holland, who was standing nearby.

"This is the last butternut squash," I said.

Horrified, Holland gasped, "In the world?"

Unfinished

This is a true story.

There was this guy.

He built his wife a little home by the side of the road, and when it was finished, they moved in and lived there happily—for a little while. Neat and trim it was, but homey it was not. After just a little while the man's wife left the little home—and him.

Distraught, he confided to a friend that the little home haunted him with memories of her.

"Remove everything that reminds you of her," was the friend's advice.

So, he did.

With her gone, the little house stood still and quiet, but the inside was moving. The man moved all her personal items out to anywhere but there, and eventually, he completely emptied the house. Little by little, boxful by boxful, it all went away:

The pictures hung by her hand,
the knick knacks she had placed,
the bed where she'd slept,
the chair that had held her, the footstool, too,
the dishes she'd touched,
the kitchen in which she'd cooked,
the rugs she'd stood upon,

the tub where she'd bathed,
and even the doorways she'd stood in.

All the things that his mind's eye could picture her near, he removed. But still, the little house reminded him of her. He saw her in every corner of every room.

The siding disappeared.

The roof shingles went missing.

The windows vanished.

The chimney was removed.

The exterior walls were torn down.

It all went away until nothing remained.

And finally, the little home he built for her was unfinished.

So, he too went away.

And no one knows where.

Mr. Mean Buttonhead

I ate lunch at the Salem General Store, a little hole-in-the-wall that had quite a few, some right down to the laths and rockwool insulation. Hanging on the wall was a pencil drawing of a vexed man with his hair standing straight up and out sideways, each strand of hair with a button glued onto its end.

The artwork was created by Bradley, the owner's young son, and was a rendition of Bradley's father, who, according to four-year-old Bradley, had been "a meanie" on that particular morning. Bradley had gone to school and learned about the letter B, and therefore, had had a box of buttons at his disposal.

Not to be bested by Bradley, Mr. Mean Buttonhead framed his likeness and hung it in a prominent spot in his business for the purpose of payback when Bradley reaches the age of embarrassment, adding his own penciling on the bottom: "by Bradley."

I could have stayed home and eaten in my own kitchen and minded my own business, but if I did, I would never meet folks like Bradley and Mr. Mean Buttonhead, which I prefer.

Think Tank and Hillbillies

Marguerite was an executive for a think tank in Washington, D.C. The goal of this pool of intelligence was to solve the problems of the world. Once a problem was identified, it became Marguerite's job to locate the best global experts on the subject and then, if necessary, get them to the United States. So, using her international connections she sifted through hundreds, if not thousands, of geniuses and decided which brain is larger than the problem. Her biggest problem was getting the thinker to the tank. Now, it doesn't take a genius to deal with geniuses, but after listening to Marguerite's stories, I'm convinced it obviously takes a mastermind.

For instance, one worldly whiz kid, after receiving his airline tickets, decided he needed a trip to Bogatell Beach in Barcelona for a few days before his brain could stew in a tank in Washington. He told Marguerite he'd come to Washington after a couple of days of R&R on the beach. This was not acceptable, of course, so Marguerite used her skills to get him here ASAP. Whether she used enticement, encouragement, bribery, threats, treats, or something else, she would not say, for doing so would give away a highly secret method. She only said, with a mischievous grin, that she managed to get the left-brained playboy on the right continent minus a Spanish tan.

She also told me about the time she battled the immigration services for several weeks because they did not want a particular unscrupulous smarty in our country. Finally, out of frustration, she called the muscle men in the State Department. The smarty was sitting in the tank the very next day.

"Seems like a lot of unnecessary work to me," I told her. "You only need to go to the bar at Trails End Steak House up in Eustis during happy hour. The world's problems are solved daily between four and six o'clock."

We also had a three-year-old sweetie from Regan, Tennessee, here. She brought her entourage—her stuffed toys, her hair ribbons, her barrettes, and her parents. This couple, a Southern Baptist minister and his first-grade schoolteacher wife, stopped hoping for a child after fourteen years of trying, only to have Madeline in year fifteen. Madeline had a thick Tennessee accent.

"I'm tar'd," Madeline said.

"You can sleep in the car," her mother answered.

"I thank ma dawg masses may."

"Your puppy is having a wonderful time at Grandma's."

Madeline doesn't like to have her hair combed and was rather vocal on the subject one morning. Her southern manners flew out the northern window of her room, and she cried out in unintelligible twangy objections. Her mother swatted Madeline's butt and said, "Hold still while I brush! If you have messy hair, they'll think we-all are hillbillies."

The preacher, his Southern belles, and the think-tank filler sat across from one another at the table, and the conversation flowed across that bridge, proving being a hillbilly might be a bad thing, but diversity is not, and once again, my breakfast table confirms that.

No think tank necessary.

A Family, a Truck Stop, and a Thanksgiving Meal

Three of my sisters and their numerous children, my parents and grandparents and a couple of cousins—met at Dysart's Truck Stop for our Thanksgiving meal. We are thankful to have each other and all that mushy rubbish, but mostly this was a gathering of convenience—we all happened to be hungry and in the vicinity of this particular truck stop. Being November is reason enough to call it our family Thanksgiving dinner, even though most of us ordered breakfast. I had the Kitchen Sink Breakfast Burrito with salsa and sour cream thrown in.

Our family stretches across Maine—from Greenville to Portland, Bangor to Dixfield—and I, being the only sane one, live in Stratton. Since our growing clan is nearly at the point of being innumerable, we don't often congregate. When we do, it's quite simply an appalling sight to behold.

Upon arriving, we clogged the truck stop entrance as we greeted one another. The other would-be customers stood outside in the rain, looking at us helplessly through the window, and knocking on the water-streaked glass doors with pleading expressions on their soggy faces. I gave and received so many hello hugs that an imprint of my glasses that were tucked into the neckline of my shirt stayed on my chest the rest of the day.

Our gathering was quite an experience for the truck stop staff. Because there are never any place cards at these impromptu family affairs, one is apt to end up sitting at the end of the table opposite from the person they most need to talk with, and just as certain to sit as far away as possible from everyone who should be on the same bill. The poor waitress inevitably ends up crouched in a corner, traumatized and mumbling, "Blub, blub, blub."

Our family get-togethers are always an embarrassingly boisterous celebration, but this time we were so loud, we muffled the engines of the hundred or so eighteen-wheelers in the parking lot. We took up three large tables and a third of the waitstaff.

My forty-something sister prefers to avoid the confusion at the adult table, opting instead for the mayhem at the kids' table, where there are at least a dozen children ranging in ages from three to forty something. They build jelly package towers and wear the plastic bread baskets as hats. They draw pictures of giraffes in hamster cages and whine about being so hungry they are surely going to die at any moment. This dramatic declaration of imminent death causes the more gullible youngsters to wail in fear and hide under the table just beyond adult reach. The older, more sinister cousins stare, eyes and smiles alive with excitement that they are about to witness the demise of a cousin.

There is never a dull moment or lapse in the conversation, especially when everyone's conflicting version of the same childhood becomes the topic. Over the years and with incessant retelling, the stories' aging foundations have crumbled beyond recognition, until not even the matriarch or patriarch can remember which kid did what to which kid. Like who pushed our sister down the stairs while she was sitting on her tricycle and who pushed her out of the car while it was in motion. It is notable, however, that no one asks why it was constantly that particular sister being pushed. I've always known this family is strange, but now, hearing our stories take on bizarre twists from obviously twisted memories, I wonder if I have wandered into a bunch of strangers.

There are those subjects that have become running discourses with no end—our mother, for instance. I remember the day she gathered us together and told us, "If I ever become screwy like your grandmother, fill my pants with rocks and throw me in the middle of Moosehead Lake."

We have the rocks, but not the courage to tell Mama it's time.

Whether you're in your dining room or at a truck stop—whether there are two of you or two dozen—matters not. What is important is the knowledge that these wacky, obnoxious, overbearing people who embarrass you and drive you absolutely nuts are the folks God thought you fit with perfectly.

So enjoy and be thankful.

A Year's Promise

My grandson, Aiden, comes to visit us often in Stratton. He loves it here—the woods, the mountains, the streams, the wildlife, and the lilac tree out front. He climbed up to a sturdy branch and sat there, not doing anything in particular except jumping me when I came around the corner of the house. He looked sort of like a partridge perched up there. I needed to remember to not let him do that anymore come bird season.

My daughter, Holland, thirteen when we moved to Stratton, wasn't so enthralled with this small-town-in-the-wilderness life. My transition to the country had been like the water that flows over the rocks in Alder Stream—a few small rapids here and there, but for the most part, an easy, meandering process. However, Holland struggled a bit. She grew up mostly in the city and was accustomed to taking drama, voice, and dance classes. She attended plays at the University of Maine. The Bangor Mall was her home away from home.

The first time Holland and I visited Fotter's Market in town, she stopped at the entrance expecting the automatic door to open for her. The doors didn't move. She put her hands on her hips and complained, "This is broken!"

I reached out and pushed on the handle and the door swung wide. So, yes, moving to the country had been a bit of adjustment for her.

When Aiden visited, he found a new little friend that lived across Stratton Brook from us. They watched each other toss crab apples in the water. That turned into a match—who could throw one completely across the brook? That turned into a friendship. They tried to get acquainted from opposite shores when finally, the other kid yelled, "I'm coming over!" and with a smile, he jumped in the water and swam across to our place. You should have seen the look on our faces. I decided we should ask him to stay for dinner.

After I asked, he threw an apple at the kitchen window of his home and when his mother opened it, he told her the plan. "And I'll throw another apple when I'm coming home so you can watch for me," he called to her. She nodded and closed the window.

Holland said, "Mom, ask him what the kids around here do for excitement."

"Mostly we throw crab apples into the brook," was his answer. "But sometimes my big brother Frankie gets in the water and acts as a target for me." You should have seen the look on Holland's face. As she walked towards the house, I heard her mumble to herself, "Oh—My—God!"

I decided then that we needed to discuss this. I asked her to give this new adventure one year. After a year, if she still didn't want this lifestyle, she could go live where she wanted, with either of her older sisters who were twenty and twenty-two years old, out on their own, living and thriving in the Bangor area, or with her father in Greenville. She agreed. One year.

That year was tough at times, but she was brave. She was faithful to her promise to give it time and was rewarded with a lifestyle she fell in love with and still lives, all these years later. She learned to fish, she learned to hunt, she drove a snowmobile to school. She learned to snowboard at Sugarloaf ski Rrsort and eventually became an Alpine Certified Level 3 ski and snowboard instructor and taught at both Sugarloaf and Saddleback ski resorts, even after graduating from high school when she could have returned to the city and city ways. But she didn't; she stayed. The first year she was old enough to vote, she had to climb down from her tree stand to do so.

I will always be so thankful she stayed.

Berries, Iodine, Myst, and Bones

Maine is wearing her favorite cloak this early morning: fog. It's thick as molasses and whitewashes the backyard. I went out to check the raspberries and was three feet off the porch before I realized it (Yes, it's an old joke).

The berries are ripe and ready to harvest for my "Out Back" raspberry jam. There aren't any berries from my knees to the ground because the dog sucks them off the bush. Sadie is my ripeness indicator. When she starts eating them, I start harvesting.

I've heard we're going to have a sad blueberry season due to poor weather. But I found a secret patch far back in the woods where the only competition is the bears. The blueberries there are as fat as my thumb and plump as my life, and worth the threat of a mauling. If the season is fruitful, my "Broken Back" blueberry jam will make it to the winter guest table, if the season is poor, it stays in the kitchen for the family.

There is an Appalachian Trail hiker here as a guest. His trail name is Iodine. As I write this, I can hear him limping around upstairs. His knee is sucking in a deep breath so it can blow, but he's on the last leg of the trail and hobbles on. Soon he will be limping down the stairs for breakfast.

There is also a hiker here nick-named Bones and another one named Myst. They too are AT through hikers. These hikers appear on my doorstep in summer and autumn, and at this late juncture on the trail (the last 280 of over 2,000 miles) they all look like Mysts and Bones.

Hobbit stayed here a few days ago. She is an itty-bitty thing and earned her trail name because she was often seen sitting on stumps having a snack. I have also hosted Jon-on-the-Mountain, Chaos (his pack was a continual unorganized mess), Chief, and The Preacher. They all hike through carrying heavy packs and short stories, and I will never tire of having the world's wanderers arrive at my door. Even the stinky ones.

November Leaves

It was fall when I met him. He was bundled up in a parka. The parka was so big, it doubled his size. He had the hood pulled tight over his wool hat. He wore a scarf around his neck and big, bulky mittens on his hands that were tucked deep inside his parka pockets. It was forty degrees outside.

"You're not from around here, are you?" I asked. He said he was from Florida and added, "I had this chance to see Maine, but I didn't want to be cold."

"This isn't cold," I countered. "It's not cold until it's freezing."

And just to brag, I offered a history lesson. "The coldest recorded temperature in this state was minus fifty. It hit that low on January 16, 2009, at the Big Black River up near the Canadian border. Fifty degrees below zero! Now, that's cold." (The old record was minus forty degrees, set in 1925 up in "The County" in Van Buren.)

I wasn't judging this guy, it's just that our bodies were obviously in different seasons.

Now it is almost November. The temperature is below forty degrees. The skies are threatening to snow. This is the reason Maine loses a lot of folks this month every year. They drain the cabin pipes, close it up, pack up, and head south. That's what November does to many Mainers. Some have already left. The hang-on-ers and fall foliage appreciators are so often asked, "When are you heading out?"

that they are starting to think they should wear a T-shirt that reads, "First Week in November."

It's time to say goodbye to the lakes and ponds where they spend their summers. It's time to listen to the surf one last time and then say goodbye. It's time to bring in the hummingbird feeders and hammocks. Now is the time to winterize the boats, haul the docks out of the water, and store the water toys.

I'm about to join a whole bunch of other snowmen and snow-women and spend the winter enjoying it. I'll spend many days at Sugarloaf and Saddleback, local ski resorts where, even though there is snow from heaven on the ground, they make more with machinery at night while we're sleeping. That sounds a little crazy, doesn't it? Yup, it is, but we're crazy like that. We're crazy about snow, snow games, and snow toys. We live on snow and we need snow to live.

The definition of vember is this—an adrenaline rush (to the south?) or something that makes you nervous, neurotic, or uptight. November makes a lot of folks jumpy, right out of state, but in December (and the rest of winter) there is no vember in my heart.

See you soon, fellow "Snow Flakes."

See you next year, summer people.

Baby Steps to an Empty Nest

My nest is empty. When Holland, the youngest of my three daughters, turned eighteen and graduated from high school, it took her until October to move into her own place. Then it took her until the first of January to complete the move by cleaning out her belongings. She didn't go far—just down the road to a new place. A young adult still taking baby steps. The only thing left in her room is an empty dresser with missing knobs, a miniature Zen Garden because she couldn't think of how to pack the sand, pennies on the floor, a single earring back stuck between the floorboards, a huge hole in the wall, and a bigger one in a mother's heart. I sure do hate to see her go.

This was the child, who, for her first six years, whenever I left to make a quick trip to the store or to get the mail, screamed and cried and carried on like one of those over-dramatic actresses in a silent movie. Only she wasn't silent on the matter. I can still see her in my mind's eye—voice wailing and arms flailing—rehearsing what I called her death throes—throwing herself onto the couch as skillfully as any melodramatic actress throws herself into her part. Then, being emotionally destroyed, she would disintegrate into a rejected, brokenhearted bundle of killjoy that slid off the cushions onto the floor, a pathetic, sobbing heap of overreaction.

Her separation anxiety came to a screeching halt, but I'm not sure when that happened. Somewhere along the growth chart the lines changed from, "Don't leave me, Mommy! I need you!" to "I'm leaving, Mom. Can I charge a tank of gas to you?"

As Holland worked on clearing her room, she sorted through her stuff and as she worked, she made piles—stuff to take with her, stuff to wash, stuff to store, stuff to give to her sisters, stuff to give to me, stuff to give to those in need, and finally the pile of stuff that was never hers to begin with that needs to go back to the true owners. (I stuffed this particular pile of stuff into a stuff sack and stuffed it into a corner of the attic because I know I'll never find the owners of this stuff!) Holland's room is empty, but the hall, the attic, the kitchen, the laundry room, and my bedroom are in shambles—full of piles of adolescent abandon.

She didn't finish the job; she left for work, which left me to pick over and then pick up those piles. I hope to be finished weeding through this child's garden by May.

The dishwasher was proof of my fledgling chick. Instead of cereal bowls and pizza plates, it was full of coffee cups and wine glasses. The medicine cabinet also told the tale: Wrinkle cream has replaced the acne cream.

For Holland, it was a new beginning on her own, in her own place. For me, it was a return to a place where I've been before, a long time ago in a previous century. If I had the young mind I had then, perhaps I could remember what it was like. They were quiet days of no kids to fail to control, no boo-boos to bandage, no crushes to try to understand, no curfews to sleep through, and no conferences at school to roll my eyes at.

I never thought the *joie de vivre* of young blood was better replaced by the creaks of an empty house or old bones, but I'm slowly warming up to the idea of being an empty nester. Perhaps I might even become a snowbird. I won't go too soon, and it won't be for long and not too far away—perhaps just down the road. Holland might still need me, so, when I do go, it will be with baby steps.

Afterword

Closed for the Season

I was standing in front of the barn, thinking, planning, figuring, weighing pros and cons, when my phone rang.

The year was 2015, the bed-and-breakfast was an established business that kept me busy from December until spring thaw washed the skiers and the snowmobilers off the trails. The bakery was also in full swing and growing. I was baking twenty pies a day and selling them all. The buckles, the cobblers, the crisps, the breads, the jams, the jellies, planting, weeding, harvesting and processing the garden defined my life from Memorial Day to Thanksgiving. I would bake molasses cookies all day Sunday and Monday, then sell out in an hour Tuesday morning at the Rangeley Farmers Market. Bottom line: I could not keep up with demand—a known death sentence for a business.

That is why I was standing in front of the barn that had only housed my winter firewood, the garden/yard implements, and a bunch of junk. I was thinking of turning it into a sit-down bakery.

That would mean massive renovations with expensive equipment, researching and meeting new state regulations, hiring employees, and meeting a payroll. It meant paperwork. I dislike paperwork. It would mean a bigger business, but also a bigger anchor around my ankles. Those were the thoughts swirling around when my phone rang. It was my oldest daughter with the wonderful news that she was going to have a baby. Emily, daughter number two, would call with the same news a few weeks later.

Aiden had been my only grandchild for fifteen years. He was now eighteen, and three more grandsons had arrived in the past two years—grandsons I didn't see very often. Now, there were more babies on the way. My daughters had come off the rivers (Kelly was a river guide) and were back on the mainland (Emily had worked on a lobster boat on Swans Island). Their adventure now was building families. Even Holland would have her first child in the fall of that next year. She had married a Greenville man, a Maine Guide, so had stopped returning to these mountains each winter to work at the ski resorts.

I walked around the yard, the gardens; I sat along the brook and watched the beavers. The young had grown and were no longer living on the bank—they had left this stream for other waters. Perhaps that is what I should do. I remembered something my father once said to me, "The only permanent thing in life is change."

For fifteen years, I loved this life. I loved this home, this town, these people, this adventure. I had lived it to the fullest, and as much as I had loved it, it was not time to go bigger, it was time to go home—home to the grandbabies. I sold the bed-and-breakfast in April.

Hattie Mae (Miss Mae) was born in January, Cosette Joye (Cozy) was born in March, and Aldan Ervin was born in October 2016. I was there to rock them.

A friend who knows I don't twiddle my thumbs well said, "I know you're not going to spend the rest of your life in a rocking chair, so what will you do next?"

I told her, "I have some stories to tell."

About the Author

Lew-Ellyn Hughes is an eight-time winner of the Maine Press Association's Better Newspaper Contest for her column Away With Words. She grew up all over the US, but always spent her summers on Moosehead Lake. In 2001, she left her job as a nurse in Bangor to open up a bed-and-breakfast in a nineteenth-century farmhouse, chronicling her experiences as she learned how to manage guests, open a bakery, and fall in love with a small town and its people. She currently lives in Greenville.